AA

50 WALKS IN

Suffolk

50 WALKS OF 1–10 MILES

First published 2003
Researched and written by Tony Kelly
Field checked and updated 2009
by David Hancock and Clive Tully

Commissioning Editor: Sandy Draper
Senior Editor: Penny Fowler
Designer: Tracey Butler
Picture Research: Liz Stacey
Proofreader: Pam Stagg
Cartography provided by the Mapping
Services Department of AA Publishing

Produced by AA Publishing
© AA Media Limited 2009

Published by AA Publishing (a trading
name of AA Media Limited, whose
registered office is Fanum House, Basing
View, Basingstoke, Hampshire RG21 4EA;
registered number 06112600)

  This product includes
mapping data licensed
from the Ordnance Survey® with the
permission of the Controller of Her
Majesty's Stationery Office. © Crown
Copyright 2009. All rights reserved.
Licence number 100021153.

A03628

ISBN: 978-0-7495-6294-2
ISBN: 978-0-7495-6327-1

A CIP catalogue record for this book
is available from the British Library.

The contents of this book are believed
correct at the time of printing.
Nevertheless, the publishers cannot be held
responsible for any errors or omissions or
for changes in the details given in this book
or for the consequences of any reliance on
the information it provides. This does not
affect your statutory rights. We have tried
to ensure accuracy in this book, but things
do change and we would be grateful if
readers would advise us of any inaccuracies
they may encounter.

We have taken all reasonable steps to
ensure that these walks are safe and
achievable by walkers with a realistic level
of fitness. However, all outdoor activities
involve a degree of risk and the publishers
accept no responsibility for any injuries
caused to readers whilst following these
walks. For more advice on walking safely
see page 144. The mileage range shown
on the front cover is for guidance only –
some walks may be less than or exceed
these distances.

Visit AA Publishing at theAA.com/bookshop

Cover reproduction by Keenes
Group, Andover
Printed by Printer Trento Srl, Italy

Acknowledgements
The Automobile Association would like
to thank the following photographers,
companies and picture libraries for their
assistance in the preparation of this book.

Abbreviations for the picture credits are as
follows: (t) top; (b) bottom; (l) left; (r) right;
(c) centre; (AA) AA World Travel Library.

3 AA/T Mackie; 9 AA/T Mackie; 18/9 AA/P
Davies; 30/1 AA/T Mackie; 56/7 AA/T
Mackie; 66/7 AA/T Mackie; 110/1 AA/T
Mackie; 124/5 Photolibrary Group; 140/1
AA/C Sawyer.

Illustrations by Andrew Hutchinson

Every effort has been made to trace the
copyright holders, and we apologise in
advance for any accidental errors. We
would be happy to apply any corrections in
the following edition of this publication.

Author acknowledgement
The author would like to acknowledge the
support staff at Suffolk County Council,
the National Trust and West Stow Country
Park, especially Kate Sussams at Sutton Hoo
and the rangers at West Stow, who came
to the rescue when he had locked himself
out of his car. He would also like to thank
his wife, Kate and son, Adam, for putting up
with his absences and accompanying him on
the walks at Southwold and Thorpeness.

Right: Colour-washed houses near the beach at Aldeburgh, Suffolk (Walk 7)

50 WALKS IN

Suffolk

50 WALKS OF 2–10 MILES

Contents

Contents

Rating
Each walk is rated for its relative difficulty compared to the other walks in this book. Walks marked ✚✚✚ are likely to be shorter and easier with little total ascent. The hardest walks are marked ✚✚✚.

Walking in Safety
For advice and safety tips see page 144.

Locator Map

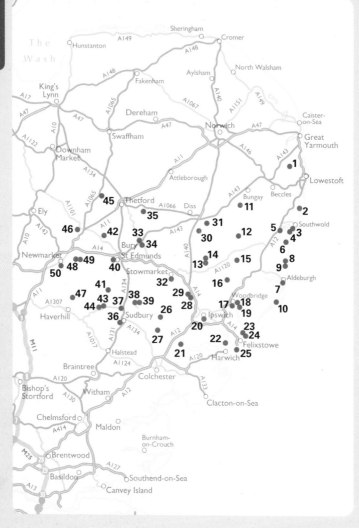

Legend

--→--	Walk Route		Built-up Area
❶	Route Waypoint		Woodland Area
- - - -	Adjoining Path	🛉🛉	Toilet
⚡	Viewpoint	P	Car Park
•	Place of Interest	🎋	Picnic Area
⌂	Steep Section	)(	Bridge

Introducing Suffolk

Suffolk, people will tell you, is flat. It is true that its highest point is just 420ft (128m) above sea level, but this is what gives Suffolk its wide open vistas, its huge sunsets and its famously sweeping skies. And although there are no mountains to climb, with very little effort you can be up on a ridge enjoying endless views over rolling countryside punctuated by pretty villages and medieval church towers.

For walkers, the easternmost county of England also offers surprising variety. Within an hour of the Cambridgeshire–Suffolk borders, you can be walking among farmland, heathland, forest, river valleys, estuaries and coast. Much of the countryside has been given over to intensive agriculture, but there are still plenty of hedgerows, ponds and marshes, attracting birds and other wildlife, as well as interesting towns and villages to explore.

This is the land of the 'South Folk', the Anglo-Saxons who arrived in East Anglia after the departure of the Romans and established their first settlements at places such as Gipeswic (Ipswich) and West Stow. You can still feel the pull of these early English ancestors as you stand beside the burial mounds at Sutton Hoo or on the cliffs at Dunwich, a once great city that has tumbled into the sea. This is also the land that has inspired countless writers and artists over the years. The bucolic landscapes of the Stour Valley are still as John Constable painted them, and on a windswept day at Aldeburgh you can almost hear the poetry of George Crabbe and the music of Benjamin Britten coming in on the waves.

The walks in this book have been chosen to capture the essence of Suffolk in all its diversity. You will visit medieval wool towns such as Lavenham and Long Melford, with their timber-framed houses and magnificent churches built by wealthy 15th-century merchants. You will discover picture-book villages, from Somerleyton in the north to Kersey in the south and Cavendish and Dalham in the west. You will explore the great tidal estuaries of the Deben, Orwell and Stour, and the peaceful river valleys of the Blyth, Gipping and Lark. You will follow the coast from disappearing Covehithe to bustling Felixstowe. On three town trails you will discover maritime Ipswich, the Georgian splendour of Bury St Edmunds and the sights associated with horse racing in Newmarket. And, just to show that Suffolk has its industrial, modern side, there are walks beside Mildenhall airfield, Felixstowe docks, Sizewell nuclear power station and the strange military architecture of Orford Ness.

PUBLIC TRANSPORT

Call Traveline East Anglia on 0871 200 22 33, or use the online journey planner at www.travelineeastanglia.co.uk for details of all bus and rail services in the county. There are good bus connections between Ipswich and the major towns, but services to outlying villages are infrequent so you will need to plan ahead or take a car. The walks at Somerleyton, Woodbridge, Ipswich, Stowmarket, Sudbury, Bury St Edmunds, Brandon and Newmarket all start close to railway stations and there is also a station at Needham Market which can be used as an alternative start point for Walks 28 and 29. National Rail Enquiries can be contacted on 08457 484950.

Most of these walks can be completed in half a day, and there are suggestions for where to spend the rest of the day, from museums to country pubs. Each main walk also has a theme for you to think about as you walk. The main obstacles encountered by walkers in Suffolk are nettles (which means trousers rather than shorts are a good idea) and paths blocked by ploughing or overgrown crops. For this reason many of the walks make use of the excellent network of long-distance trails and short circular walks in Suffolk, which tend to be well maintained and signed. Although there are more than 3,000 miles (4,800km) of public rights of way in Suffolk, you will sometimes find it easier to use permissive paths, where the landowner is committed to access, or minor country roads, than to fight your way across a field of prickly corn or oilseed rape.

Using this book

Information Panels

An information panel for each walk shows its relative difficulty (see page 5), the distance and total amount of ascent. An indication of the gradients you will encounter is shown by the rating ▲ ▲ ▲ (no steep slopes) to ▲ ▲ ▲ (several very steep slopes).

Maps

There are 30 maps, covering 40 of the walks. Some walks have a suggested option in the same area. The information panel for these walks will tell you how much extra walking is involved. On short-cut suggestions the panel will tell you the total distance if you set out from the start of the main walk. Where an option returns to the same point on the main walk, just the distance of the loop is given. Where an option leaves the main walk at one point and returns to it at another, then the distance shown is for the whole walk. The minimum time suggested is for reasonably fit walkers and doesn't allow for stops. Each walk has a suggested map.

Start Points

The start of each walk is given as a six-figure grid reference prefixed by two letters indicating which 100km square of the National Grid it refers to. You'll find more information on grid references on most Ordnance Survey maps.

Dogs

We have tried to give dog owners useful advice about how dog friendly each walk is. Please respect other countryside users. Keep your dog under control, especially around livestock, and obey local bylaws and other dog control notices.

Car Parking

Many of the car parks suggested are public, but occasionally you may find you have to park on the roadside or in a lay-by. Please be considerate when you leave your car, ensuring that access roads or gates are not blocked and that other vehicles can pass safely.

Right: Trees in silhouette on the River Blyth (Walks 3 and 4)

A Victorian Eccentric at Somerleyton

A walk around the delightful estate village designed by a flamboyant Victorian railway magnate.

DISTANCE 6.25 miles (10.1km)	MINIMUM TIME 2hrs 30min
ASCENT/GRADIENT 131ft (40m) ▲▲▲	LEVEL OF DIFFICULTY +++

PATHS Farm tracks, field-edge paths, country lanes, 2 stiles

LANDSCAPE Farmland, village and River Waveney

SUGGESTED MAP OS Explorer OL40 The Broads

START/FINISH Grid reference: TM 484972

DOG FRIENDLINESS On lead across farmland, off lead on Waddling Lane

PARKING On-street parking outside Somerleyton post office

PUBLIC TOILETS At marina

The story book of Suffolk is filled with interesting characters but few had a more colourful life than Sir Samuel Morton Peto (1809–89) of Somerleyton Hall. At the age of 21, he took over his uncle's building business and he went on to become one of the great Victorian entrepreneurs. Together with his cousin, Thomas Grissel, he was responsible for many of the most familiar public buildings in London, including Nelson's Column, the Houses of Parliament, several theatres, hospitals, prisons and even the brick sewers that are still in use today.

Great Victorian Entrepreneur

Despite this, his first love was railways and he is best remembered as one of the pioneers of steam locomotion. During his lifetime he built more than 750 miles (1,206km) of railway line in Britain and 2,300 miles (3,700km) abroad, from Canada to Russia and Australia. During the Crimean War (1854-56), he built the world's first military railway at Balaclava, completely without profit, an act for which he was rewarded with a knighthood.

He is also remembered locally as the father of modern Lowestoft. It was he who turned a small fishing village into a busy port with the construction of a harbour for 1,000 boats, and he built seaside hotels and a holiday resort on deserted marshes and scrubland. He built the railway link from Lowestoft to Norwich, opening up the town's fishing trade and fulfilling his promise that the morning catch from Lowestoft would arrive in Manchester in time for tea. The railway line still survives and there is still a station at Somerleyton, the village he made his own.

Somerleyton Hall

In 1843, Sir Morton Peto purchased Somerleyton Hall. He proceeded to rebuild this Jacobean mansion in the Anglo-Italian style favoured by wealthy Victorians and transformed the parkland. At the same time, he built the thatched red-brick estate cottages for his workers which contribute so much to the village's charm. He also provided the village with an unusual thatched school, which must be the prettiest school in

SOMERLEYTON

Suffolk. The village as you see it today is almost totally the creation of Sir Morton Peto and his eccentric tastes in architecture.

Sir Morton also found time to be the Liberal MP for Norwich for 20 years. However, in the best tradition of flamboyant entrepreneurs, it all went wrong in the end. In 1866, he was declared bankrupt with unpaid debts of one million pounds. Somerleyton Hall was bought by the carpet manufacturer Sir Francis Crossley, whose son became the first Lord Somerleyton. His great-grandson, the present Lord Somerleyton, still lives in the hall and can be seen riding around his estate on misty mornings.

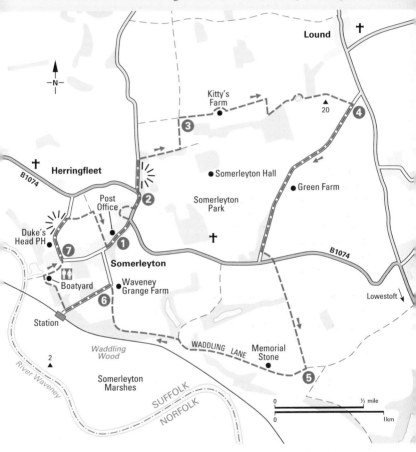

WALK 1 DIRECTIONS

❶ With the post office behind you, turn left and walk past estate cottages towards the village green. Turn left to walk around the green and continue around the outside of the school. Return to the road, turn left and walk along the pavement opposite the red-brick wall of Somerleyton Park.

❷ Follow this road round to the left and turn right on a lane signposted 'Ashby'. There are glimpses of Somerleyton Hall across parkland to your right. After 300yds (274m), turn right past a thatched lodge at the pedestrian entrance to Somerleyton Hall. Pass through the gates and keep on this lane for 400yds (366m), then turn left on to a field-edge path.

3 After 300yds (274m), turn right on to a farm track. Stay on this waymarked path as it swings left through the farmyard and continues alongside two fields, then turns sharp right towards a wood. Turn left to walk along the edge of the wood and keep to the path as it bends around a pond and enters a small belt of woodland. Keep right through the woods and cross a stile, then look for the second gap in the hedge to your right and bear half left on a cross-field path to reach a hedge and lane on the other side.

4 Turn right and stay on this lane for 1 mile (1.6km). Just before a road junction, take the field-edge path to your left and follow this round to a gap in the wall. Cross the B1074 and climb a stile to keep straight ahead on a field-edge path for almost 0.75 mile (1.2km).

WHAT TO LOOK OUT FOR

On Waddling Lane, look out for the small memorial stone to American airmen Lt J Black and Lt T Aiken, who died when their plane crashed here while returning from a mission in November 1944.

5 Turn right at the end of this track along Waddling Lane. The path drops down towards the water-meadows with the railway and River Waveney to your left. When the path divides, fork left to climb around the edge of Waddling Wood. Keep straight ahead when a track joins from the left to head uphill and away from the woods.

6 Turn left opposite Waveney Grange Farm and walk down towards the station. Turn right opposite the station entrance on a wide track. When the track bends right, keep left on a grassy path

WHERE TO EAT AND DRINK

The Duke's Head serves pub meals and has large gardens and a children's play area. Teas are served in the courtyard garden of the post office in summer.

to drop down to a boatyard. Turn left around the boatyard buildings to reach a marina, then turn right past the marina and climb the access drive to a road.

7 Turn left and walk along the pavement as far as the Duke's Head pub. Stay on this road as it bends to the right with views of round-towered Herringfleet church over the hedge to your left. At the next bend, by the black railings of a cottage, turn right on a waymarked path. Follow this path along the edge of the field and turn right beyond a telegraph pole, past a row of houses. At the kissing gate, turn left to return to the start of the walk.

WHILE YOU'RE THERE

Somerleyton Hall and Gardens are open on certain days in summer, usually Thursday and Sunday. The hall contains fine state rooms and carved woodwork, while the gardens are famous for the yew hedge maze, planted in 1846. There is also a loggia tea room serving light lunches and afternoon teas, and a miniature steam railway which young children will enjoy.

The Crumbling Cliffs of Covehithe

*See the effects of coastal erosion at first hand
as you walk along a rapidly disappearing cliff top.*

DISTANCE *4.5 miles (7.2km)*	MINIMUM TIME *1hr 45min*
ASCENT/GRADIENT *131ft (40m)* ▲▲▲	LEVEL OF DIFFICULTY +++
PATHS *Cliff top, shingle beach, farm track and country lanes, 1 stile*	
LANDSCAPE *Farmland, woodland, cliffs, sea, lagoon*	
SUGGESTED MAP *OS Explorer 231 Southwold & Bungay*	
START/FINISH *Grid reference: TM 522818*	
DOG FRIENDLINESS *On lead across nature reserve and beach*	
PARKING *On street near Covehithe church*	
PUBLIC TOILETS *None en route*	

Nowhere else in Suffolk do you feel the power of the sea so much as on this walk along the cliffs at Covehithe. Coastal erosion is threatening much of East Anglia, but here the sea is advancing at the rate of almost 10yds (9m) a year. The ground is being swallowed up from under your feet and the beach is littered with the debris of collapsed trees. This is definitely not a walk for those with a fear of heights.

Coastal Erosion

Come here soon because this landscape will probably not be here in 50 years' time. Right along the coast of north Suffolk the tides are eating away at the cliffs, depositing the shingle further south on Orford Ness. This is a process which has been going on for thousands of years, part of the natural realignment of the coastline which has already seen most of Dunwich disappear beneath the waves. But rising sea levels, caused by global warming, and the extraction of sand and gravel from the seabed, to feed the demand for new homes and roads, have accelerated the erosion to the point where Covehithe will soon be little more than a memory.

Thatched Church

The small village is dominated by St Andrew's Church, whose tall tower has long been a beacon to sailors. Built in the 15th century, when Covehithe was perhaps 2 miles (3.2km) from the shore, the church was always out of all proportion to the population of a village which never exceeded 300 people and is now down to fewer than 30. In 1672 the roof was dismantled and a smaller church was built within the ruins, using material stripped from the earlier structure. The thatched church now stands beneath the original tower, a beautiful sight but one whose days are numbered.

From the church, a tarmac road leads to the edge of the cliffs and then suddenly comes to an abrupt end, forcing you to wonder what once lay beyond. Stern notices warn you not to continue, but in fact there is a well-used concessionary path along the edge of the cliffs. Each year the path is pushed further inland as valuable farmland is lost to the encroaching tides and the few remaining houses edge closer to the sea. Try to imagine, as you walk along the cliffs, that the path you are walking on will probably not be here next year. It's not a very comforting thought.

WALK 2 DIRECTIONS

❶ Take the tarmac lane from the church down towards the sea. You reach a barrier with a 'Danger' notice and a sign warning that there is no public right of way. Although this is strictly true, this is a well-established and popular path stretching north towards Kessingland beach and you are likely to meet many other walkers. The warnings are serious but it is quite safe to walk here so long as you keep away from the cliff edge.

❷ Walk through the gap to the right of the road barrier and continue towards the cliffs, then turn left along a wide farm track with a pig farm to your left.

WHERE TO EAT AND DRINK

There are no facilities of any kind on this walk, so you need to take a picnic and eat it on the beach or among the ruins of the church at Covehithe. The nearest pubs are the Five Bells and the Horse and Groom, both in the nearby village of Wrentham.

The path follows the cliff top then drops down towards the beach to enter the Benacre nature reserve. On the left is Benacre Broad, once an estuary, now a marshy lagoon. Like others on the Suffolk coast, the shingle beach here attracts little terns in spring and summer and you should keep to the path to avoid disturbing their nesting sites.

3 Climb back on to a well-worn path on the cliffs at the end of Benacre Broad. The way cuts through pine trees and bracken on a constantly changing path before running alongside a field and swinging right to drop back down to beach level where you should take the wide grass track on your left across the dunes.

4 When you reach a concrete track, with the tower of Kessingland church visible in the distance, turn left following the waymarks of the Suffolk Coast and Heaths Path. Go through a kissing gate and keep straight ahead, passing Beach Farm on the right. Stay straight ahead for a mile (1.6km) on a wide track between the fields with views of Benacre church up ahead.

5 Go through some steel gates and turn left on to a quiet country lane. Stay on this lane for 0.75 mile (1.2km) as it passes between hedges with arable farmland to either side and swings left at the entrance to Hall Farm.

6 When the road bends right, turn left past a gate. Stay on this path as it swings right around a meadow and continues into the woodland of Holly Grove. Pass through another gate and turn left along the road for the last 0.75 mile (1.2km) back into Covehithe. Turn left at the junction to return to the church.

From Sunny Southwold and its Pier

*Around this old-fashioned holiday resort
on an island surrounded by river, creek and sea.*

DISTANCE 4 miles (6.4km)	**MINIMUM TIME** 1hr 30min
ASCENT/GRADIENT Negligible ▲▲▲	**LEVEL OF DIFFICULTY** ✦✦✦
PATHS Riverside paths, seaside promenade, town streets, 2 stiles	
LANDSCAPE Southwold and its surroundings – river, marshes, coast	
SUGGESTED MAP OS Explorer 231 Southwold & Bungay	
START/FINISH Grid reference: TM 511766	
DOG FRIENDLINESS Most of walk suitable for dogs off lead	
PARKING Beach car park (pay-and-display) or free in nearby streets	
PUBLIC TOILETS Beside pier, near beach and car park at Southwold Harbour	

The arrival of the first steamboats for more than 70 years marked a return to the glory days for Southwold Pier in the summer of 2002. The pier was originally built in 1899, when Southwold was a flourishing Victorian holiday resort. Mixed bathing had just been introduced on the beach, on condition that men and women were kept at least 20yds (18m) apart and changed in separate 'bathing machines' into costumes which covered their bodies from neck to knees. The *Belle* steamer brought holiday-makers on its daily voyage from London and the pier was a hive of activity as porters unloaded their cases and carried them to their lodgings.

Pleasure Pier

The T-end, where the boats docked, was swept away in a storm in 1934. During World War Two, the pier was split in two as a precaution against a German invasion. By the time Chris and Helen Iredale bought the pier in 1987, storms and many years of neglect had reduced it to a rotting hulk. Years later, the couple have realised their dream of rebuilding and reopening the pier, so that visitors can once again stroll along the boardwalk with the sea spray in their face,s and watch the boats unloading their passengers at a new landing stage.

Old-fashioned Fun

An exhibition on the pier tells the history of the traditional British seaside holiday, complete with saucy postcards, kitsch teapots, palm readers, end-of-the-pier shows, high-diving 'professors' and old-style arcade machines – such as the 'kiss-meter' where you can find out whether you are flirtatious, amorous, frigid or sexy.

A separate pavilion contains modern machines by local inventor Tim Hunkin, who also designed the ingenious water clock, with chimes and special effects every half hour. You can eat ice cream or fish and chips, drink a pint of the local beer, play pool in the amusement arcade or watch the fishermen while taking in the sea air. Especially in summer, the pier provides a focus for good old-fashioned fun.

SOUTHWOLD

Not So Brash

Southwold, situated on an island between the River Blyth and the sea, is one of those genteel, low-key seaside resorts where, in spite of the pier, everything is done in good taste. Make no mistake, this is a popular spot but it has none of the brashness of kiss-me-quick Felixstowe or Lowestoft. The character of Southwold seems to be summed up by the rows of brightly-coloured beach huts on the seafront promenade – some of which have been sold for the price of a three-bedroom cottage elsewhere – and the peaceful greens with their Georgian and Edwardian houses. Adnams brewery dominates the town and it is no surprise to discover that the beer is still delivered to pubs on horse-drawn drays. Southwold is that sort of place.

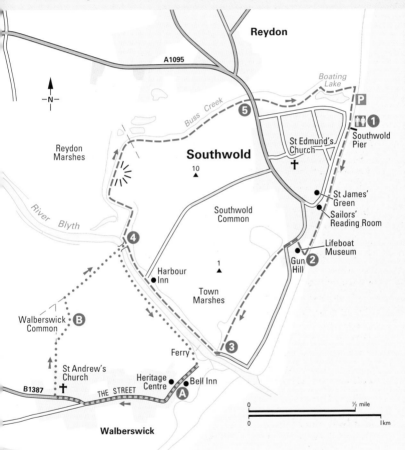

WALK 3 DIRECTIONS

1 Leave the pier and turn left along the seafront, either following the promenade past the beach huts and climbing some steps or walking along the clifftop path with views over the beach.

After passing St James' Green, where a pair of cannon stand either side of a mast, continue along the clifftop path to Gun Hill, where six more cannon, captured at the Battle of Culloden near Inverness in 1746, can be seen facing out to sea.

Overleaf: Multi-coloured bathing huts line the beach at Southwold (Walk 3)

WALK 3

2 From Gun Hill, head inland alongside the large South Green, then turn left along Queen's Road to the junction with Gardner Road. Cross this road, then look for the Ferry Path footpath, that follows a pleasant stream beside the marshes as it heads towards the river. Alternatively, stay on the clifftop path, and walk across the dunes until you reach the mouth of the River Blyth.

WHAT TO LOOK OUT FOR

It's worth a visit to the cathedral-like St Edmund's Church, whose 100ft (30m) flint tower stands guard over the town. The greatest treasure here is the 15th-century rood screen which spans the width of the church, a riot of colour as vivid as when it was painted, with angels in glory and a set of panels depicting the twelve apostles.

3 Turn right and walk beside the river, passing the Walberswick ferry, a group of fishing huts where fresh fish is sold, and the Harbour Inn. After about 0.75 mile (1.2km),

WHILE YOU'RE THERE

The Southwold Sailors' Reading Room on East Cliff was opened in 1864 in memory of Captain Rayley, a naval officer at the time of the Battle of Trafalgar. Although it still retains its original purpose as a library and meeting place, it is now a small museum containing model boats, figureheads and portraits of local sailors and fishermen. Nearby, on Gun Hill, a former coastguard look-out houses the tiny Lifeboat Museum, open on summer afternoons, with exhibits on the history of the Southwold lifeboats. Among the items to look for is a hand-operated foghorn, similar in appearance to a set of bellows.

you reach an iron bridge on the site of the old Southwold-to-Halesworth railway line.

4 Keep straight ahead at the bridge, crossing a stile and following the path round to the right alongside Buss Creek to make a complete circuit of the island. There are good views across the common to Southwold, dominated by the lighthouse and the tower of St Edmund's Church. Horses and cattle can often be seen grazing on the marshes. Keep straight ahead, going over a stile, through a gate to cross an embankment, then over another stile. Stay on the raised path to reach a white-painted bridge.

WHERE TO EAT AND DRINK

There are numerous cafés and restaurants in Southwold, many of them specialising in fresh local fish. Sutherland House, on the High Street, serves fresh fish and game in the setting of an Elizabethan merchant's house, used by the Duke of York (later James II), Lord High Admiral of England, as his headquarters during the Battle of Sole Bay, when the British and Dutch fleets clashed off Southwold in 1672. Among the pubs serving Adnams beer are the Sole Bay Inn, a Victorian pub opposite the brewery on East Green, and the Red Lion on South Green. Another good choice is the Harbour Inn, beside the river at the half-way point of the walk.

5 Climb up to the road and cross the bridge, then continue on the path beside Buss Creek with views of beach huts in the distance. The path skirts a boating lake on its way down to the sea. Turn right and walk across the car park to return to the pier.

Across the River to Walberswick

A longer walk from Southwold, crossing the River Blyth to the artists' village of Walberswick.
See map and information panel for Walk 3

DISTANCE 4.5 miles (7.2km) or 6 miles (9.7km) if ferry not running

MINIMUM TIME 2hrs

ASCENT/GRADIENT 98ft (30m) ▲▲▲   **LEVEL OF DIFFICULTY** ✦✦✦

WALK 4 DIRECTIONS (Walk 3 option)

Turn right at Point ❸ and look for the landing stage, where a ferryboat shuttles back and forth across the river in summer. At various times this route has been served by a steamboat and a chain ferry, but these days you travel in an old-fashioned rowing boat for which you pay a modest charge. You may catch a glimpse of an old man and boy, waiting for the last ferry. The spectral couple are the ghosts of a pair who drowned whilst trying to cross the river. In winter, when the ferry does not operate, stay on the main route until you reach Point ❹, then cross the bridge and walk back along the path on the other side of the river, adding 1.5 miles (2.4km) to the walk.

On the opposite bank, keep straight ahead to walk along The Street through Walberswick. You pass the Bell Inn on your left and come to the village green, Point ❹, where a heritage centre, situated inside an old chapel, features displays on the history of the village. In the 15th century, this was a thriving port with a large fishing fleet. When the harbour silted up, Walberswick went into decline and it is only recently that it has discovered a new lease of life as an artists' colony and a popular trip for holiday-makers from Southwold who take the ferry and spend the afternoon browsing in its tea rooms, art galleries and antiques shops.

Stay on The Street as it bends right and fork right at a junction to reach St Andrew's Church, built within the ruins of an earlier church which stands as a testament to Walberswick's changing history. Just beyond the church, turn right along Church Street and follow this lane to the end. Keep straight ahead on a path across Walberswick Common, an area of gorse and open heathland. When the path forks, keep right and follow this path to a tarmac lane, Point ⓑ.

Turn left and stay on this lane as it bends right on the old trackbed of the Southwold-to-Halesworth railway. Continue until you reach an iron footbridge, Point ❹ of the main walk. Cross this bridge and turn left to continue with Walk 3.

Snape Maltings

From Maltings to Sandlings

DISTANCE 7 miles (11.3km)		MINIMUM TIME 2hr 30min
ASCENT/GRADIENT 85ft (26m) ▲▲▲		LEVEL OF DIFFICULTY +++
PATHS Riverside embankments, forest track and country lanes		
LANDSCAPE Estuary, farmland, forest		
SUGGESTED MAP OS Explorer 212 Woodbridge & Saxmundham		
START/FINISH Grid reference: TM 392575		
DOG FRIENDLINESS On lead		
PARKING At Snape Maltings		
PUBLIC TOILETS At Snape Maltings		

WALK 5 DIRECTIONS

At its height, Snape Maltings was one of the largest flat floor maltings in the country, with 7 acres (2.8ha) of buildings. In the 19th century, 100-ton sailing barges would pull into the quay here to take malt made from Suffolk barley to breweries in London and Norwich. But such large complexes were inefficient, and in 1965, after 120 years, the malting of barley ceased, and the owner began converting the buildings to other uses.

The initial development turned the malthouse into a concert hall, which subsequently has become famous the world over as the home of Benjamin Britten's Aldeburgh Festival. It was opened in 1967, but was gutted by fire two years later on the first night of the festival. It was completely restored within a year, and is now used for other concerts as well as the annual Aldeburgh Festival.

Other buildings were converted, initially to provide an art gallery and craft shop, but now there is a whole complex of shops and refreshment places. Renovation and conversion continues, with other buildings being turned into flats.

This route gives you a good look at the different landscapes which make up the Suffolk Coastal belt known as the Sandlings, all part of the Suffolk Coast Area of Outstanding Natural Beauty. From the Maltings car park, turn left on to the B1069 road, and at the junction with a road signposted to Orford, go left on to a broad green track with a Suffolk Coast Path (SCP) sign.

WHERE TO EAT AND DRINK

Everything you could want is at Snape Maltings. The Granary Tea Shop and Metfield Deli and Café serve teas, snacks and light lunches,. The Plough and Sail pub dates back to the 16th century, when it was a smugglers' inn. Today, the traditional bar has an adjacent modern restaurant, which serves dishes using many ingredients from the Farmers Market, where local produce is available for sale on the first Saturday of every month.

SNAPE MALTINGS

The track heads towards the marshes at the edge of the river, with Snape Maltings and car park beyond the hedge to your left. The path joins another track coming in from the left, turning parallel to the river, and heading for a thin line of trees, where the path becomes boardwalk, with fields to your right, and reeds lining the river bank to your left. Walk along the bottom edge of Iken Cliff picnic site, a sloping field with views across the river, and continue to follow the SCP markers. Along the Alde Estuary you may see a variety of wetland birds such as avocet, redshank, shelduck and grey heron.

Go right up some steps, then following a path between two fences. Turn left on to a sandy track, and after about 100yds (91m), right on to a tarmac road, looking for a footpath sign to the left after another 100yds (91m). Follow this broad track down to the buildings of a pig farm, bearing left around the buildings and through the car park, then right on to a track heading up a shallow hill towards some trees. Carry straight on when you reach the corner of the wood, then go right and then left to take you on to a broad track on the other side of the line of trees.

The track goes through a line of trees ahead, and when you get to the other side, take the footpath right, still following the SCP blue discs with yellow arrows. With trees to your right, and a wide expanse of pig enclosures to your left, continue ahead to a road.

Cross the road to the right and take the SCP signed footpath leading to the left. Head into the Tunstall Forest to reach a fork in the path after about 100yds (91m). The left path continues with the

SCP. Follow the other path, which from now on takes you more or less straight ahead through the forest as you cross other junctions. The narrow path widens out, and crosses a number of forestry tracks before arriving at a clearing with some forestry cottages. You may notice that the Tunstall Forest is far from typical. Apart from conifers, you'll see a variety of broadleaved trees, gorse, and open heathland, home to rare ground-nesting birds such as the nightjar and woodlark

Continue in the same line across the corner of the clearing, crossing a gravel track and taking the wide grassy path to the right of a post bearing the number 30. The path crosses a minor road, then shortly after emerges on to the edge of Blaxhall Heath, where you may see some of the long ditches dug during the Second World War to foil German glider landings. This part of the route is a long distance path called the Sandlings Walk, denoted by posts with a black arrow and nightjar symbol. Cross the B1069, and continue straight ahead around a black and yellow forestry gate. The trees are rather younger here, mainly silver birch.

The path narrows down, and, at the point where it meets a minor road, turn right and follow the road back to Snape Maltings.

WHILE YOU'RE THERE

It may be tempting to spend most of your time at Snape Maltings in the shops – everything from antiques to speciality conserves and beer – and refreshment places. But spare some time to wander around the sculpture lawn, behind the complex of buildings, next to the river. Here you'll find massive sculptures by Henry Moore, Barbara Hepworth and Alison Wilding in an unsurpassable setting.

The Ghosts of Dunwich

Conjure up visions of a lost city as you stand on the cliffs gazing out to sea

---

DISTANCE 8 miles (12.9km) **MINIMUM TIME** 4hrs

ASCENT/GRADIENT 262ft (80m) ▲▲▲ **LEVEL OF DIFFICULTY** +++

PATHS Farm tracks, heathland paths, quiet roads, shingle beach

LANDSCAPE Heathland, woodland, farmland, marshes and coast

SUGGESTED MAP OS Explorers 212 Woodbridge & Saxmundham; 231 Southwold & Bungay

START/FINISH Grid reference: TM 479707 (on Explorer 231)

DOG FRIENDLINESS On lead on National Trust land and Dingle Marshes

PARKING Dunwich Beach free car park

PUBLIC TOILETS At car park

Medieval Dunwich was a splendid city and a major seaport that exported wool and grain to Europe and imported cloth and wine. It had six churches plus numerous chapels, convents, monasteries, hospitals, alehouses, farmhouses and mills. Now it is a small seaside village with a handful of houses and a pub. So where has it gone? The answer is that, like so much of the Suffolk coast, it has simply vanished into the sea.

The sea has been the making and breaking of Dunwich. It was the sea that provided the very reason for its existence and supported its industries of shipbuilding and fishing. It was the sea that brought its most famous figure, St Felix of Burgundy, a missionary invited by King Sigebert, to preach Christianity to the pagans of East Anglia and rewarded with a bishopric and a cathedral at Dunwich in AD 630. It was the sea that silted up the harbour during a terrible storm in 1286, leading to the city's inevitable decline. And it is the sea, ever since, which has taken Dunwich back, a process which continues at the rate of around 1yd (1m) each year as the tides chip away at the base of the cliffs.

A scale model of the 12th-century city, housed in Dunwich Museum, reveals the full truth about its decline. The Roman town here extended 1 mile (1.6km) out to sea beyond the present coastline. Half of this had disappeared by the time of the Norman conquest but the worst was yet to come. The last church tumbled over the cliffs as recently as 1920 and the museum has a series of dramatic photographs showing it collapsing year by year. According to a local legend, you can still hear the bells of the sunken churches pealing beneath the sea on a stormy night.

This walk also takes you to Dunwich Heath, where the National Trust manages some 215 acres (87ha) of sandy cliffs and a mile (1.6km) of beach as a conservation area. The area was once part of the extensive Sandlings Heaths and consists of miles of excellent walks and tracks through open heathland. It borders the RSPB's Minsmere Nature Reserve and the shady woods and expanses of heather attract a wealth of birdlife, including Dartford warblers and nightjars. Come, if you can, between June and September, when the heathland on the cliff top is carpeted with glorious purple and pink heather.

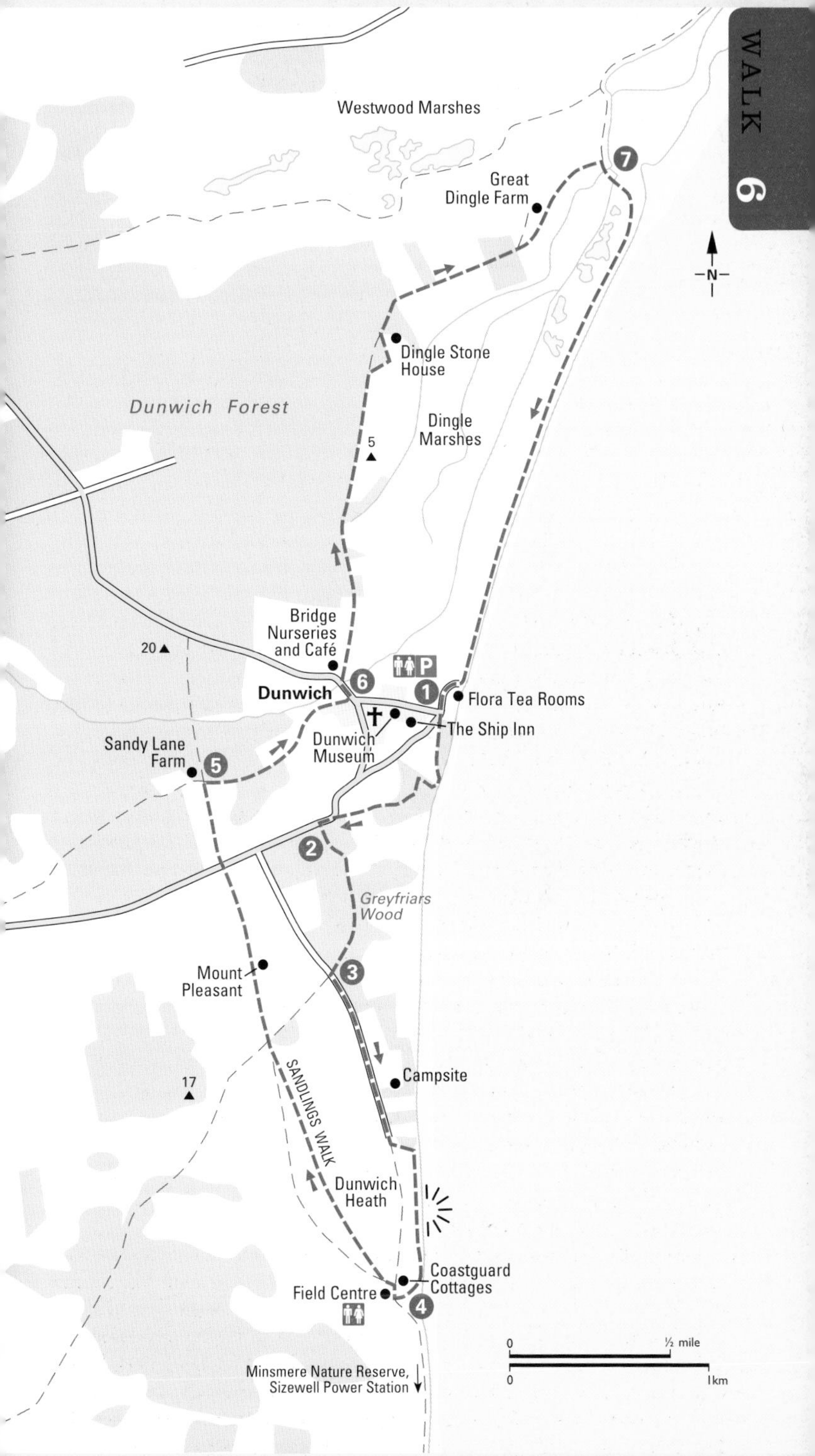

WALK

6

Westwood Marshes

Great
Dingle Farm

7

-N-

Dingle Stone
House

Dunwich Forest

Dingle
Marshes

5

Bridge
Nurseries
and Café

6

1

Flora Tea Rooms

Dunwich

The Ship Inn

Dunwich
Museum

Sandy Lane
Farm

5

20

2

Greyfriars
Wood

Mount
Pleasant

3

17

Campsite

SANDLINGS WALK

Dunwich
Heath

Coastguard
Cottages

Field Centre

4

Minsmere Nature Reserve,
Sizewell Power Station

0   ½ mile

0   1km

WALK 6 DIRECTIONS

1 Walk up the road from the beach car park and keep left at the junction. When the road bends, turn left on to a footpath that climbs through the woods to the ruins of Greyfriars Friary. Turn left along the cliff top, go over a set of wooden steps and bear right through the trees on a waymarked path. At the end of this path, turn right along a track to a road.

2 Turn left off the road after 100yds (91m) on a track to the Dairy House. Keep straight ahead on this path as it enters Greyfriars Wood and continues to a road.

3 Turn left and walk along this road for 0.5 mile (800m), passing two caravan sites on the left. As soon as you enter National Trust land, turn left on to a path waymarked with white arrows.

4 Walk around the National Trust's Coastguard Cottages and take the track beside Heath Barn

field centre, then bear right on to a sandy path that climbs through the heather. Keep on this path, bearing left and right at a crossing track to follow the Sandlings Walk nightjar waymarks. When you reach a bridleway, keep straight ahead on a farm track passing Mount Pleasant farm. Cross the road and keep straight ahead on a concrete lane to Sandy Lane Farm.

5 Turn right for 0.5 mile (800m) on a shady path to emerge by St James's Church, built in the 19th century when Dunwich's other churches were falling into the sea. For a short cut, keep straight ahead here to return to Dunwich.

6 Turn left at the road and, in 100yds (91m), go right at Bridge Nurseries and Café. Keep to the right around the farm buildings and stay on this track for 1.5 miles (2.4km) beside Dunwich Forest before turning seawards. Pass through a gate to enter a covert and fork right at a junction around Great Dingle Farm, then follow the path through the reed beds towards the sea.

7 Turn right at a junction when you see an old drainage mill to your left, and follow the flood bank across Dingle Marshes. Turn right to return to Dunwich along the beach or take the path behind the shingle bank.

Benjamin Britten's Aldeburgh

A walk in the footsteps of Britain's best-known 20th-century composer.

DISTANCE *5.75 miles (9.2km)*   MINIMUM TIME *2hrs 30min*

ASCENT/GRADIENT *Negligible* ▲▲▲   LEVEL OF DIFFICULTY ✚✚✚

PATHS *River and sea wall, meadows, old railway track*

LANDSCAPE *Town, river, marshes and beach*

SUGGESTED MAP *OS Explorer 212 Woodbridge & Saxmundham*

START/FINISH *Grid reference: TM 463555*

DOG FRIENDLINESS *Off lead on river wall, on lead on permissive path – not allowed on beach between May and September*

PARKING *Slaughden Quay free car park*

PUBLIC TOILETS *Slaughden Quay, Fort Green, Moot Hall*

Aldeburgh is one of those places that has been put on the map by one man. In medieval times this was a busy port with fishing and shipbuilding industries, but in a story which has been repeated up and down the Suffolk coast, its harbour silted up and it went into decline as the River Alde was diverted southwards by the shingle bank of Orford Ness. Today, Aldeburgh is buzzing once again and the cafés on the seafront are full of excited chatter as visitors come in their thousands to pay homage to the town's most famous resident, Benjamin Britten.

Britain's Leading Composer

Britten (1913–76) was the leading British composer of the 20th century and the man who introduced many people to classical music through works like *The Young Person's Guide to the Orchestra* and his opera for children, *Noye's Fludde*. Born in Lowestoft, the son of a local dentist, he grew up with the sound of the sea and began composing at the age of five. During World War Two he moved to the United States as a conscientious objector, and it was here that he first read the work of George Crabbe (1754–1832), an Aldeburgh poet. Crabbe's father was a salt-master and two of his brothers had been lost at sea.

It was through Crabbe that Britten rediscovered his Suffolk roots. He returned to Snape to write *Peter Grimes*, an opera based on Crabbe's poems about the gritty lives of Aldeburgh fishermen. If ever a piece of music had a sense of place, this is it. You hear the waves breaking on the shingle beach, the seagulls swooping over the coast, the wind coming in on the tide. The leading role was created for Britten's lifelong partner and collaborator, the operatic tenor Peter Pears.

Aldeburgh Festival

Benjamin Britten's most lasting contribution to Aldeburgh was the foundation of the Aldeburgh Festival, which he achieved together with Pears and the librettist Eric Crozier in 1948. A number of Britten's best-known works were first performed at the festival, including *Noye's Fludde*, *Curlew River* and *A Midsummer Night's Dream*. At first the concerts took place in local churches and the Jubilee Hall, but eventually a larger venue was needed. In 1967, the festival was moved to a new concert hall at Snape Maltings, a 19th-century granary outside Aldeburgh that now hosts musical events throughout the year and not just during the main festival in June. Britten and Pears continued to live in Aldeburgh, initially in a seafront house on Crabbe Street and later in a large farmhouse on the edge of town. They are buried side by side in the churchyard of the parish church of St Peter and St Paul.

WALK 7 DIRECTIONS

❶ Start at Slaughden Quay, once a thriving port, now a yacht club. Walk back briefly in the direction of Aldeburgh and turn left along the river wall on the north bank of the River Alde. There are good views to your left of the Martello tower that marks the northern end of Orford Ness. Stay on the river wall for 2 miles (3.2km) as the river swings to the right towards Aldeburgh.

❷ When the river bends left, go down the wooden staircase to your right and keep straight ahead across a meadow with a water tower visible ahead. Go through a gate and bear half-left across the next meadow to cross over a footbridge. Next, follow the waymarks, bearing half right, then keep straight ahead across the next field to come to another footbridge. After crossing a fifth footbridge, the path runs alongside allotments and goes through a gate to reach a lane.

③ Turn left by a brick wall and cross the recreation ground. Continue past the fire station to reach a road. Turn right for 75yds (69m) then go left on a signposted footpath almost opposite the hospital entrance. Follow this path between houses, cross a road and keep straight ahead with a caravan site on the right.

④ When you see a footpath on the right, leading to a track across the caravan park, turn left and immediately right on a permissive path that follows the trackbed of an old railway. Stay on this path for 0.5 mile (800m) as it climbs steadily between farmland to the left and woodland and marshes to the right. Turn right at a junction of paths to reach the open meadows. Stay on this path, crossing the North Warren nature reserve with views of Sizewell power station to your left.

⑤ Cross the road and turn right along a tarmac path that runs parallel to the beach. As you approach Aldeburgh, you pass a striking scallop sculpture on the shingle (erected in 2003 to celebrate Benjamin Britten's life in Aldeburgh), fishermen's huts and fishing boats that have been pulled up on to the shingle. Pass the timber-framed Moot Hall and continue along Crag Path, past a lifeboat station and a pair of 19th-century look-out towers. At the end of Crag Path, bear right across a car park and walk around the old mill to return to Slaughden Quay.

Sizewell A, B...
and Sea

*The unexpected delights of a circuit
around a controversial nuclear plant.*

DISTANCE *6.75 miles (10.9km)*   **MINIMUM TIME** *3hrs*

ASCENT/GRADIENT *164ft (50m)* ▲▲▲   **LEVEL OF DIFFICULTY** ✦✦✦

PATHS *Footpaths, coast path, short stretches of road, 2 stiles*

LANDSCAPE *Sizewell power station and its surroundings*

SUGGESTED MAP *OS Explorer 212 Woodbridge & Saxmundham*

START/FINISH *Grid reference: TM 475629*

DOG FRIENDLINESS *Be aware of wildlife and nesting birds on beach*

PARKING *Sizewell Beach car park (free in winter)*

PUBLIC TOILETS *Sizewell Beach*

Taking a walk around a nuclear power station may seem like a strange idea, especially to those who come from that generation of students whose windows were plastered with stickers proclaiming 'Nuclear power? No thanks.' Yet this walk in the shadow of Sizewell B is a special one. It has wetland, woodland, heathland, farmland and a section of unspoilt coast, with the surreal sight of the white dome of the power station as an ever-present backdrop.

Sizewell B is probably the most controversial building in Suffolk. The first gas-cooled reactor, Sizewell A, opened in 1966, but it was the appearance of the 'golf ball' at Sizewell B that prompted a wave of protests and one of Britain's longest public enquiries. This is the only pressurised water reactor in Britain and it began operating in 1995 when memories of nuclear disasters at Chernobyl and Three Mile Island were still fresh. The hemispherical dome is 148ft (45m) in diameter and 213ft (65m) tall, protected by concrete walls designed to withstand a nuclear accident or an earthquake.

The land around the power stations, owned by British Energy, is managed as a nature reserve in conjunction with Suffolk Wildlife Trust, and there is a network of waymarked walks that you can follow across woodland and grazing marshes. Orchids grow in the meadows in early summer, bluebells appear in the woods in spring and dragonflies and damselflies buzz around the marshes. Some of the few pairs of black redstart in Britain have even started to nest on the power station buildings.

An alternative walk takes you to Thorpeness, a fairy-tale village created by Glencairn Stuart Ogilvie after he purchased the Sizewell Estate in 1910 and transformed the fishing hamlet of Thorpe into a holiday resort. The chief attraction is The Meare, an artificial boating lake with islands and play houses themed around the story of Peter Pan. Ogilvie wanted to create a slice of 'Merrie England' – there is a golf course, a country club, mock-Tudor houses and numerous architectural follies including the delightful House in the Clouds. This cleverly designed water tower, built to supply the water pump across the road, was disguised as a timber-framed house and has become the dominant feature of the Thorpeness skyline, appearing, from a distance, to be lodged in the trees. It is now a charming holiday home.

Minsmere
Nature Reserve

Minsmere Level

Minsmere New Cut

—N—

Eel's Foot
PH

Eastbridge

4 Eastbridge
Farm

Ruined
Chapel

5 Sluice

76 ▲

Upper Abbey

Goose Hill

Kenton Hills

P

Sizewell Belts
Nature Reserve

3 Reckham
Lodge

Sizewell B ●

Leiston

▲
15

Sizewell A ●

1 **P**
Sizewell
Beach Café
● Sizewell
2 ● The Vulcan
Arms PH

Campsite ●

● Sizewell Hall

Dismantled Railway

D

Aldringham

B1353

Aldringham
Common

▲
12

A

House in the
Clouds

Golf
Course

Mere
Cottage

C

B

† Thorpeness

Thorpeness
Country Club

The Meare

0   ½ mile

0   1 km

WALK 8

WALK 8 DIRECTIONS

1 Walk up the road away from the beach or cross the meadow behind the car park and cross a stile to reach the Vulcan Arms. Continue along the road past the entrance to the power stations. Turn right after 400yds (366m) on to a track and stay on this track for 300yds (274m).

> ### WHAT TO LOOK OUT FOR
> Kittiwakes are a species of seagull with white heads, grey wings and black legs. They usually breed further north but a colony of some 200 breeding pairs has been established since 1996 on the offshore rigs near Sizewell A.

2 Turn left just before a cottage and follow this path beneath the power lines and alongside a small wood on the left. Cross a stile beside a gate and continue across the open meadow with views of Sizewell B to your right. A path on the right leads into the Sizewell Belts nature reserve (no dogs). Keep straight ahead on a wide bridle path. Cross a stile, then where the path swings left, turn right and immediately left beside Reckham Lodge to cross an area of heathland

3 At a meadow and fork of paths, bear half right, drop down through bracken to a footbridge

> ### WHERE TO EAT AND DRINK
> The Sizewell beach café is open from Wednesday to Sunday throughout the year and makes a good place for a pot of tea or a plate of fish and chips. A wider range of food and drink is available at the Vulcan Arms pub, near the start of the walk. There is also the Eel's Foot, situated just off the walk in the village of Eastbridge.

and cross a meadow to another footbridge. Cross duckboards and continue through trees to a track. Turn left, then left again to reach the car park for the permissive walks. Turn right on to a track and continue ahead for 0.75 mile (1.2km), following it left at a cottage to meet a road. Turn right to walk into Eastbridge.

4 After passing Eastbridge Farm on the left, look for a footpath on the right, signposted 'Minsmere Sluice'. After 50yds (46m) the path swings sharp right then turns left beside a hedge and continues alongside a field. Pass through a belt of trees and stay on this narrow footpath across the fields with views over the Minsmere Level to your left. Pass through two gates to cross to the far side of a ditch and continue on a grassy lane. The path eventually swings left to run alongside the New Cut, with views of the Minsmere Nature Reserve to your left and the strange sight of Sizewell B juxtaposed behind a ruined chapel to your right.

> ### WHILE YOU'RE THERE
> Take time to explore the network of trails which have been set up on the land around the power stations in an effort to convince the public that nuclear energy is eco-friendly. There are two sets of walks, the Kenton and Goose hills woodlands (dogs on lead) and the Sizewell Belts nature trails (no dogs). You can pick up free maps at the car park near Point **3** on the main walk.

5 Turn right at Minsmere Sluice to return to Sizewell along a wide grass track or scramble up to the top of the cliffs. Turn right just beyond the power stations to return to the car park.

The Model Village of Thorpeness

An optional extra walk from Sizewell,
taking in the fairy-tale holiday village at Thorpeness.
See map and information panel for Walk 8

DISTANCE 5.25 miles (8.4km)   MINIMUM TIME 2hrs

ASCENT/GRADIENT 98ft (30m) ▲▲▲   LEVEL OF DIFFICULTY ✦✦✦

WALK 9 DIRECTIONS
(Walk 8 option)

Walk past the Sizewell beach café and head for the beach, then turn right across the sand dunes. After passing beneath Cliff House, the large white house on the cliffs, turn right to climb to the cliff top and turn left on the Suffolk Coast Path. Pass a campsite on the right and walk through a tunnel beneath the staircase leading to Sizewell Hall, now a Christian conference centre. Stay on the clifftop path as it drops slowly down towards the beach to run behind the shingle. When the path eventually runs out, turn right up the cliff, Point **Ⓐ**, and turn left along the clifftop path to reach a gravel track by The Red House.

Soon join the road and follow it round to the right. When you see the Dolphin pub ahead, turn left on to a track, passing the Thorpeness Country Club and its lawn tennis courts to emerge opposite The Meare, Point **Ⓑ**. In summer you can hire a rowing boat here or enjoy a cream tea by the lake.

Turn right alongside The Meare and take the second left, Uplands Road. Stay on this track as it climbs past a windmill on the left and the House in the Clouds to the right. At a golf course, keep straight ahead between hedgerows and follow this path across the course, keeping the waterways of The Meare to your left. Turn right just before Mere Cottage, Point **Ⓒ**, and stay on this path to a maintenance area, where you turn left on a gravel track to meet the main road. Cross the road and keep straight ahead, following the line of a disused railway.

When the main track bends right, keep straight ahead and go through a gate to enter a conservation area (Aldringham Walk) on a narrow path climbing through the bracken. When you reach another gate, Point **Ⓓ**, go through and fork right at a junction of paths with Sizewell B visible up ahead. Stay on this track between farmland to the left and heathland to the right. Keep straight ahead at a crossroads of paths. At a road, turn right and then left before the entrance gates to Sizewell Hall. Keep to the left of the campsite and turn left along the cliffs to return to the car park along the back of the beach.

Bombs and Bunkers at Orford Ness

An odd clash of human and natural landscapes on Europe's largest shingle spit.

DISTANCE	5 miles (8km) MINIMUM TIME 2hrs
ASCENT/GRADIENT	Negligible ▲▲▲ LEVEL OF DIFFICULTY ✦✦✦
PATHS	Paved roads and shingle
LANDSCAPE	Shingle, marshes and abandoned military buildings
SUGGESTED MAP	Guidebook and map from National Trust ticket booth at Orford Quay
START/FINISH	Grid reference: TM 425495
DOG FRIENDLINESS	Dogs not allowed
PARKING	Orford Quay pay-and-display car park
PUBLIC TOILETS	At car park and on Orford Ness

NOTE *Orford Ness can be visited only by taking National Trust ferry crossing from Orford Quay. Operates most days at height of summer and Saturdays from May to October. (Call 01394 450900 to check times.)*

WALK 10 DIRECTIONS

Of all the walks in this book, none can match the eerie appeal of this walk on Orford Ness. This is a hostile and lonely place, a shingle spit 10 miles (16.1km) long and growing at the rate of more than 15yds (14m) a year. Its isolation made it a perfect site for military testing, and for much of the 20th century, Orford Ness was a secret defence establishment where major advances were made in the fields of radar, military photography, bombs and atomic weapons. The army has gone but the buildings remain as permanent reminders of another age. Barn owls nest in the abandoned barracks. Little terns lay their eggs on the beach. The combination of wilderness and derelict buildings is strangely compelling and is what makes Orford Ness such a special place.

Arriving on Orford Ness, follow the red trail, which is waymarked with red arrows painted on to the road surface. It is essential to stick to the authorised route, not only to avoid disturbing wildlife, but also to keep out of the way of unexploded ordnance, which remains a potential danger.

The trail begins by the wall of the River Ore, looking out over marshes where cattle graze on the site of a World War I airfield. In late summer, once the birds have finished nesting, you can continue

WHERE TO EAT AND DRINK

There are no facilities on Orford Ness, so it is essential to take plenty of water. The Jolly Sailor and the King's Head both serve good local fish and chips and the Riverside Tearooms serves light lunches and teas. Butley Orford Oysterage, on Market Hill, offers oysters from its own beds as well as smoked salmon, smoked trout, oyster soup, fish pie and pork and cockle stew.

along the river on the green trail through an area of marshes and lagoons. The main trail turns away from the river at this point and heads for an information building in the former telephone exchange. Look inside at the displays on the history of Orford Ness and the large aerial photograph of the shingle spit. Behind the building is an observation platform with views over the Stony Ditch creek and the strange pagoda-type structures of the Atomic Weapons Research Establishment (AWRE), which operated here at the height of the Cold War.

Follow the trail along the High Street and bear right over a Bailey bridge to cross Stony Ditch, with salt marsh to either side. Fork right here to head for the Black Beacon, a marine navigation beacon dating from 1928. The upper floors provide displays on birdlife and there is an elevated viewing area. The road to the right leads to the laboratories where Britain's early atomic weapons were tested, although it is claimed that no nuclear material was involved. You can walk right inside Laboratory 1, where the first test took place in 1956, but the rest of the AWRE site is still out of bounds to visitors.

Return to the Black Beacon and head towards the beach, passing a police tower on the line of the old perimeter fence. Now turn left to walk along the shingle. The trail heads inland again when you come to a lighthouse and an old coastguard look-out that the National Trust plans to restore. Walk across the shingle to the Bomb Ballistics Building, built in 1933 as the nerve centre of Britain's bomb-testing programme. You can climb on to the roof for views over the Ness, stretching north towards Sizewell, south

towards Felixstowe and inland to Orford Castle. The large grey building to the north, known as Cobra Mist, was a top secret Anglo-American satellite research base alleged to have been involved in tracking UFOs (Unidentified Flying Objects) before its closure in 1973. It now houses transmitters for the BBC World Service, which also uses the tall radio masts beyond.

WHILE YOU'RE THERE

Orford Castle is a 12th-century Norman keep built by Henry II, with a spiral staircase leading to a tower offering wonderful views over Orford Ness. Orford itself is a lovely town to explore, with craft shops, smokehouses and a museum devoted to underwater exploration at Dunwich.

Walk back over the Bailey bridge and retrace your steps to the jetty. Before you leave this eerie place, try to imagine the contribution that Orford Ness has made to 20th-century British history. It was here in the 1930s that Sir Robert Watson-Watt and a small team of scientists took the first steps in the development of the air defence system which came to be known as radar. Without the work carried out at Orford Ness, the outcome of the Battle of Britain might have been different and the course of World War II may have changed. Something to think about as you take the ferry back to Orford.

The Saints of South Elmham

Wide open views and huge expanses of working arable farmland on a walk through Saints Country.

DISTANCE 8.75 miles (14.1km)   **MINIMUM TIME** 4hrs

ASCENT/GRADIENT 295ft (90m) ▲▲▲   **LEVEL OF DIFFICULTY** +++

PATHS Field paths, meadows and country lanes, 3 stiles

LANDSCAPE Arable farmland and sweeping views

SUGGESTED MAP OS Explorer 231 Southwold & Bungay

START/FINISH Grid reference: TM 306833

DOG FRIENDLINESS On lead across farmland

PARKING South Elmham Hall free car park (when closed, start from St Peter's Hall)

PUBLIC TOILETS None en route

The scattered group of parishes, which makes up South Elmham is collectively known as Saints Country. This is an area of high arable farmland, with huge skies and endless views, punctuated by little villages with the names of St James, St Margaret, St Michael, St Nicholas, St Peter, St Cross and All Saints.

Important Religious Centre

Although there is no firm evidence for this, it is believed that South Elmham was an important religious centre in Anglo-Saxon times. The walk begins at South Elmham Hall, a 16th-century moated manor house on the site of an old hunting lodge and deer park used by the bishops of Norwich. It was an 11th-century bishop, Herbert de Losinga, who built the minster here, possibly over the ruins of a 7th-century wooden church. The historian Bede refers to an Anglo-Saxon see at Elmham, which may either have been here or at North Elmham in Norfolk. We know that Felix of Burgundy arrived in Suffolk to convert East Anglia to Christianity and established his cathedral at Dunwich. South Elmham, 14 miles (22.5km) inland, would have made an obvious spot for a second church.

Environmental Improvements

The present owner of South Elmham Hall, John Sanderson, has opened the land to walkers and made a number of environmental improvements under a countryside stewardship scheme designed to ensure a balance between farming and conservation. New hedgerows have been planted and green corridors have been established alongside all of the fields, providing paths for walkers and important habitats for wildlife. Come here at dusk and you may be lucky enough to see barn owls hunting for mice and voles.

Although the route of the walk is mostly on public rights of way, there is also an extensive network of permissive paths across the farm, which means that you'll be walking across parkland, arable fields and pasture for a herd of British White cattle.

SOUTH ELMHAM

At the mid-point of the walk you have the chance to visit St Peter's Hall, a 13th-century moated farmhouse that was extended in 1539 using materials from the abandoned Flixton Priory. This magnificent house is now home to St Peter's Brewery, which produces traditional ales from local barley and malt and water from a deep borehole below the hall. Among the beers that they have revived are Suffolk Gold, wheat beer, honey porter, spiced winter ale, elderberry beer and a millennium brew dating back to the year 1000 and containing juniper and nettles but no hops. The shop is open every day for you to buy beer to take home but the best time to visit is at weekends (Friday to Sunday) when you can take a tour of the brewery and sample the beers in the lovely old bar.

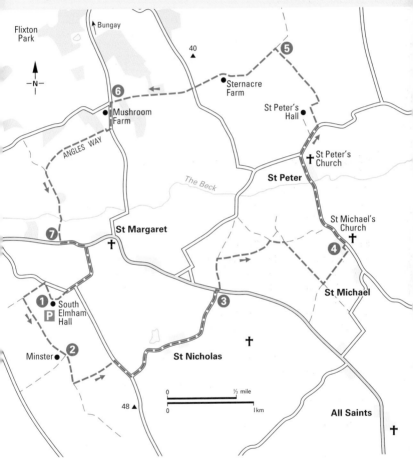

WALK 11 DIRECTIONS

❶ From the car park, walk between the trees and cross the moat on a permissive path. Take the footbridge over a stream and keep straight ahead across the meadow. Go through a gate and turn left along a green lane enclosed by hedges. At a junction of tracks, turn left to cross a footbridge and through a kissing gate. Walk across the meadows to admire the site of the minster, a romantic ruin enclosed by trees perfectly set within the landscape.

WALK 11

2 After visiting the minster, continue straight ahead along the line of the hedge and turn left at the end of the next meadow to cross a footbridge and climb on a field-edge path. Turn right at the road and after 300yds (274m) turn left on to a quiet lane. Follow this lane as it bends to the right and continue for 0.75 mile (1.2km).

3 Cross the main road and keep straight ahead on a grassy field-edge path. Pass through a hedge, cross the next field and turn right beyond the hedge. Walk beside this hedge for 0.5 mile (800m) until you come to a junction where you turn right on to a cross-field path that becomes a wide track. Turn left at a crossroads and walk across the fields with a water tower to your right to reach St Michael's Church.

4 Turn left along the road. After 0.5 mile (800m), cross a humpback bridge and stay on this road to climb to St Peter's Church. Follow the road round to the right past the entrance to St Peter's Hall, then turn left across a plank bridge to walk beside the moat. The path swings right then left, following the line of a hedge between open fields.

5 At a junction of paths, turn left along a field-edge track, waymarked 'Angles Way'. This soon becomes a grassy lane and

then a pebbled farm drive. Cross a road and keep straight ahead on a concrete track.

6 Turn left at the next road to pass Mushroom Farm and, in 300yds (274m), go right on a field-edge path. After 0.5 mile (800m), you reach a junction of paths with a half-white, half-weatherboarded farmhouse visible to your right. Turn left to climb towards a small wood and continue through the woods. Go through a gate, cross a stream, go through another gate and climb the green lane to a road.

7 Turn left, then right in 300yds (274m) on to a lane signposted 'South Elmham Hall'. Follow this lane round to the right to return to the start.

Back to the Low House at Laxfield

What better way to enjoy a summer evening than a country stroll to a Victorian pub.

DISTANCE 3.5 miles (5.7km)   MINIMUM TIME 1hr 30min

ASCENT/GRADIENT 98ft (30m) ▲▲▲   LEVEL OF DIFFICULTY ✦✦✦

PATHS Field-edge paths and country lanes

LANDSCAPE Farmland and village

SUGGESTED MAP OS Explorer 231 Southwold & Bungay

START/FINISH Grid reference: TM 296724

DOG FRIENDLINESS On lead across farmland

PARKING Church Plain, Laxfield

PUBLIC TOILETS None en route

This walk is really just an excuse to work up a good thirst before a visit to one of Suffolk's most charming pubs. The King's Head at Laxfield is usually known as the Low House because of its situation below the church and the village centre. This thatched pub, which actually dates from Tudor times, has changed little since the Victorian era when Arthur Fellgate, the village blacksmith, was landlord for 61 years before handing over the pub to two of his fourteen children. A grainy black-and-white photo of Arthur and his long-suffering wife Anna hangs in the front parlour.

A Pub With No Bar

An open fire burns in the parlour on winter evenings, and drinkers warm themselves while seated on a three-sided Victorian settle or high-backed wooden bench. To either side of the parlour are more cosy little rooms, filled with wooden tables, cushions and pews. There is no bar – the beer is served from a tap room out the back, where the landlord pours pints of Adnams bitter straight from the barrel. In summer, you can sit out of doors around a historic bowling green or take a seat inside the summer house.

Even the pub sign on the street is eccentric, featuring the head of Charles I on one side and Henry VIII on the other. This much-loved old local was threatened with closure in the 1990s but the villagers formed a consortium to buy it and it is thriving once again. Musicians play here on Tuesday afternoons and on summer evenings the gardens are the setting for Shakespearean plays. This really is the perfect place to end a walk.

Historic Village

Laxfield is a historic village whose former market square is edged on three sides by All Saints Church, the Guildhall and the 15th-century Royal Oak pub. The church is unusual in being some 36ft (11m) wide yet having a single nave and no aisles. The most impressive building is the timber-framed Guildhall, which dates from the 16th century and has since seen service as a schoolroom, a wholesale shop, a poorhouse, a reading room,

LAXFIELD

a billiard room and a working men's club. These days it houses the parish office, a doctor's surgery and a museum on the upper floor.

The walk takes you out into the countryside around Laxfield, with views of All Saints Church across the fields. Although much of the walk is on tarmac lanes rather than footpaths, there is little traffic and in this part of Suffolk this is often preferable to fighting your way along the edge of a large arable field, beating back long ears of overgrown barley, rape and wheat.

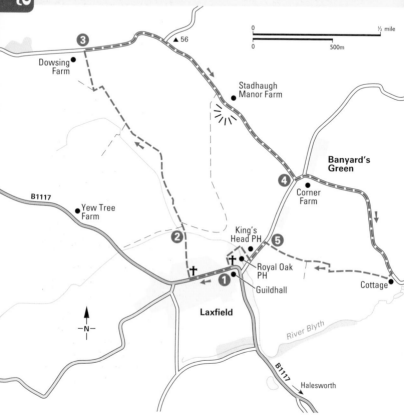

WALK 12 DIRECTIONS

❶ Start on Church Plain with the Royal Oak behind you and walk along the High Street. After passing a Baptist chapel on your right, look for a footpath on the same side of the street which runs between a hedge and a cemetery. Stay on this path as it passes beneath a green canopy and crosses a footbridge over the River Blyth. The river rises just outside Laxfield and is little more than a stream at this point.

❷ Take the left fork to reach open countryside and follow the field-edge path with a hedge to the right. Ignore all paths leading off and stay on this path to climb around the field towards a distant farmhouse. Eventually the path turns left, then right beside a ditch and then along the outer hedge of the farmhouse to reach a road.

❸ Turn right and stay on this road for 1 mile (1.6km), keeping to the right when the road divides. This is a lovely quiet country lane

WHILE YOU'RE THERE

The Laxfield and District Museum, in the Guildhall, is open on weekend afternoons from May to September and features rural and domestic bygones, a restored Victorian kitchen and village shop, and displays of local history and archaeology. A popular outing in summer is a horse-drawn carriage ride from nearby Tannington Hall, an Elizabethan manor house and hotel. Details are available at the King's Head.

WHAT TO LOOK OUT FOR

As you walk past the Baptist chapel, notice the plaque to John Noyes, who was burned at the stake on this spot in 1557. A firm Protestant, he was charged with heresy after he refused to accept the Catholic doctrine of transubstantiation, which states that the bread and wine at the Eucharist become Christ's actual body and blood.

and there are good views towards Laxfield across the huge fields to your right.

4 Turn left at Corner Farm and fork right along the lane, signposted 'Ubbeston'. After passing a stud farm, the road bends right, then narrows and starts to descend into the valley. When you see a cream-coloured cottage ahead, turn right on to a footpath. As you pass through the hedge you will once again see the tower of All Saints Church up ahead. Keep straight ahead towards a line of willow trees and continue along the edge of the field. Turn right then left to join a farm track that leads to a tarmac lane, where you should keep straight ahead.

5 When you reach a road, turn left to return to Laxfield. Take the first right to arrive at the Low House (King's Head pub) and that well-earned pint. When you are ready, turn right outside the pub and left along Church Walk, or walk through the churchyard to return to Church Plain.

WHERE TO EAT AND DRINK

Where else? The King's Head, despite its Victorian image, actually has quite a modern menu that features old favourites like sausages and mash as well as Cajun chicken and baked banana and Stilton cream. There is always a good selection of Adnams ales from the barrel. The Royal Oak, at the start of the walk, is another good village pub with parasols out on the square in summer.

Debenham Waddle

*Exploring the green lanes and pathways
around a historic county town.*

DISTANCE *6 miles (9.7km)* MINIMUM TIME *2hrs 30min*

ASCENT/GRADIENT *197ft (60m)* ▲▲▲ LEVEL OF DIFFICULTY ✦✦✦

PATHS *Field-edge and cross-field paths, country lanes*

LANDSCAPE *Arable farmland and new millennium wood*

SUGGESTED MAP *OS Explorer 211 Bury St Edmunds & Stowmarket*

START/FINISH *Grid reference: TM 174631*

DOG FRIENDLINESS *On lead across farmland*

PARKING *Cross Green free car park, High Street, Debenham*

PUBLIC TOILETS *Off Debenham High Street*

In 1778 a young man left Suffolk to seek his fortune, but he never forgot the place where he grew up. When William Franks opened his first small haberdashery shop in Wigmore Street in London, he named it Debenhams after his home town. Before long he had established a chain of upmarket stores specialising in fine silks and cottons and in 1905 the first Debenhams department store opened in London. The company now has more than 100 stores across Britain but few of their customers are aware of the origins of the name.

Debenham, near the source of the River Deben, is one of those places whose past has largely been forgotten. In Saxon times, this was where the East Anglian kings held court, and there are accounts of a great battle against the marauding Danes at Blood Field to the north of the town. In the 14th century, Debenham was one of the finest of the wool towns, and the evidence is there to see in the handsome timber-framed merchants' houses that line the High Street. Yet these days, stuck out in the middle of Suffolk, away from the coast, the main roads and the busy towns, Debenham is little more than a village. The fledgling river trickles along the streets and occasional tourists pass through to visit the teapot pottery (see While You're There) on their way to Framlingham Castle and the coast.

This walk takes you into the green lanes around Debenham, through rich agricultural country where barley and wheat are grown. Part of the walk is along an old packhorse route that delights in the name of Waddlegoose Lane. The other local name for this path is Waddledickie Lane, 'dickie' being the Suffolk dialect for donkey.

The longer walk takes you to Earl Soham, a charming village hidden away in a valley along the old Roman road. Many people stop here just to visit the pub, which sells beer from the village brewery. The brewery is housed in new premises alongside the village shop, which offers a fine range of local produce including organic cider and apple juice from Aspall Hall near Debenham. Aspall is one of the oldest family firms in England, founded by Clement Chevallier in 1728 and still run by the eighth generation of the Chevallier family. The business has remained on the same site throughout its history and the original apple press and stone trough are still at Aspall Hall. Go easy on the beer and cider, though, or you really will be waddling back along Waddlegoose Lane…

WALK 13 DIRECTIONS

1 Walk away from the High Street past the butcher and fork right at Priory Lane to cross the River Deben. Turn right at the road and, after 100yds (91m), turn left on a sloping cross-field path. Pass through a hedge and continue around the edge of a field before turning left along a country lane.

2 At a junction of bridleways, ignore the 'Circular Walk' signs and keep straight ahead on the oak-lined drive to Crows Hall, which takes its name from the Debenham family crest. Follow the waymarks around to the right of the farm, pass a bungalow and turn left beside a hedge on to a field-edge path. Go left again at the end of the field and stay on this path as it crosses a footbridge to the right around the Great Wood. After another 250yds (229m), turn left across the fields to come to a wide track signposted 'Bridle Way'. Turn right here and turn right along a lane to pass the large farm buildings of Grove Farm, then Crowborough Farm.

3 At the start of a line of telegraph poles, turn left alongside the hedge on to a grassy path. Stay on this path for 0.5 mile (800m), passing a wind pump and a pair of water towers before descending to a cottage with wooden barns.

4 Turn left along Waddlegoose Lane. Stay on this green lane for about 1.75 miles (2.8km). Where the obvious track bends right at a house, stay straight ahead on a field-edge path next to a hedge. At a junction bear right. The path is now enclosed by tall hedges, obscuring your view of the fields.

5 At the next junction, turn right along a farm track and stay on this track past a converted barn and a brick farmhouse. Turn left along the road for about 400yds (366m), then turn right on to a bridle path signposted 'Circular Walk'. After passing through a gate, the path goes around Hoggs Kiss Wood, one of 200 community woodlands created for the millennium. You can either stay on the path or walk down through the woods and meadows.

6 When you reach the end of Hoggs Kiss Wood, turn right around a group of allotments and fork right along Water Lane to reach the High Street. Turn left along the High Street to return to the start of the walk.

Earl Soham – Barley and Beer

Allow a full day for this longer walk, with lunch at a popular village pub.

See map and information panel for Walk 13

DISTANCE *9.75 miles (15.7km)* MINIMUM TIME *4hrs*

ASCENT/GRADIENT *328ft (100m)* ▲▲▲ LEVEL OF DIFFICULTY +++

SUGGESTED MAP *OS Explorers 211 Bury St Edmunds & Stowmarket; 212 Woodbridge & Saxmundham*

WALK 14 DIRECTIONS (Walk 13 option)

At Point ❸, instead of turning left, keep straight on along Grove Lane. At the end of the road, turn left and, in 60yds (55m), turn right along a field-edge path. Pass through a hedge to reach a second field. Two-thirds of the way across this field, turn left on a path and continue across the crops.

Keep straight ahead across a field, through a thicket and past a small pond. Cross a stile and keep going across the meadow to cross another stile and enter a green lane. The path bends left through a belt of trees then goes through a kissing gate to descend through an avenue of young trees to another kissing gate, and a road, Point ❹.

Turn right and walk along this road for 0.75 mile (1.2km) into Earl Soham. When the A1120 joins from the right, cross the road and stay on the pavement, passing Cobbolds Row, a terrace of timber-framed cottages named after a local brewer, and the Victoria pub.

Continue along The Street, passing the village green, post office, bowling green and tennis courts. Turn left at the village school, Point ❸, and fork left on a tarmac drive. At the entrance to Earl Soham Lodge, turn left on to a field-edge path that runs behind the village. Follow this path around the edge of a drained mere. Turn left at a telegraph pole, cross a footbridge, and stay on this path as it runs around a field and turns uphill and to the right. Turn left at a footpath sign and walk beside a tall hedge to reach the poplar-lined drive of Windwhistle Farm. Come up here on a windy day and you will see how the farm got its name.

Turn right and then left around the farm buildings to join a track that leads past an isolated dark pink cottage and drops down to a valley. Turn left beyond the trees to walk alongside a ditch on the edge of the field. Cross a footbridge through the hedge to reach a road, Point ❸, where you turn left and then right on to a wide bridle path. Ignore the first footpath turning off to your left and stay on this footpath to reach Point ❹ on Walk 13.

A Walk Around Framlingham Castle

Enjoy views of a 12th-century castle reflected in a lake and a stroll around a handsome market town.

WALK 15

DISTANCE 2.5 miles (4km)	**MINIMUM TIME** 1hr

ASCENT/GRADIENT 131ft (40m) ▲▲▲ **LEVEL OF DIFFICULTY** ✦✦✦

PATHS Town streets, country lanes, field paths, meadows, 1 stile

LANDSCAPE Framlingham town, castle and mere

SUGGESTED MAP OS Explorer 212 Woodbridge & Saxmundham

START/FINISH Grid reference: TM 282635

DOG FRIENDLINESS Keep dogs on lead

PARKING The Elms car park (free), New Road, Framlingham

PUBLIC TOILETS Crown and Anchor Lane, off Church Street

WALK 15 DIRECTIONS

This short walk begins in the historic town of Framlingham and heads out into the surrounding countryside, with views of the medieval castle and mere from all sides. From the car park, walk through the kissing gate that leads directly to The Mere, now a Suffolk Wildlife Trust nature reserve and bird sanctuary. The lake, which is fed by the River Ore, is a natural feature but it was enlarged in medieval times by the Dukes of Norfolk to improve the setting of Framlingham Castle. Keep to the left-hand perimeter fence of the reserve and you will soon have marvellous views of the castle reflected in the water.

Cross a footbridge and turn right, around the edge of the Framlingham College playing fields. Ignore a path coming from a footbridge on the right and continue around the field, crossing a footbridge at the end. Turn right along a lane at the entrance to Little Lodge Farm and follow this lane gently uphill.

Stay on the lane as it turns to the right at the gates of Great Lodge Farm. After 200yds (183m), turn right on to a field-edge path with good views of the castle up ahead and the Victorian red-brick Framlingham College to the right. Keep left alongside the hedge at a junction of paths to drop down to a footbridge. Cross this bridge and walk along the edge of the field. Turn right just before the road to continue around the field past an old World War II pill box.

At the far corner of the field, turn right between a fence and a hedge to follow the course of the old Town Ditch, part of the defensive system for Framlingham Castle. Turn right at the foot of the ditch

WHERE TO EAT AND DRINK

There are several choices on Market Hill. The Crown Hotel serves sandwiches, ploughman's lunches and hot meals. Across the square is the Tea Shop at No. 10 for tea and cakes. The Granary on Church Street is a coffee house serving lunches and afternoon teas.

and follow the path round to the left to return to the mere. Go through the gate on the left, climb a stile and cross a bridge to reach the green at the foot of the castle walls. Follow the path around the edge of the green then drop steeply down to the moat and climb the steps on the far side to the castle entrance.

WHAT TO LOOK OUT FOR

Don't miss the carved tombs inside St Michael's Church. The most extravagant is the tomb of Thomas Howard, 3rd Duke of Norfolk (1473–1554) and uncle of two of Henry VIII's wives. Also buried here are Henry Howard, Earl of Surrey (1517–47), Thomas' eldest son and the earliest writer of 'Shakespearean' sonnets, who was executed for high treason; and Henry Fitzroy, a son-in-law of Thomas and illegitimate son of Henry VIII.

Framlingham Castle was built in the 12th century by Hugh Bigod, whose ancestors had been granted the manor of Framlingham in return for their support during the Norman conquest. The Bigod family became Earls of Norfolk and ruled much of East Anglia as their own personal fiefdom from their castles at Bungay and Framlingham. The castle was successfully besieged by King John in 1215 but since then it has rarely been attacked. It was here that Mary I, Mary Tudor, was staying in 1553 as she waited to hear whether she or Lady Jane Grey had been declared queen after the death of Edward VI. Since then the castle has been used as a prison, a poorhouse and a school.

The castle is now administered by English Heritage and you can walk the full length of the parapet walls and climb some of the 13 towers

for views across the mere. The entry price includes an audio tour and also a museum of local history with a display on medieval moats.

Leave the castle by taking the bridge across the moat and walk past the car park to the Castle Inn. Turn left at the duck pond and walk along Castle Street. Turn right along Double Street, a crescent-shaped street on the site of the old moat, noting the Victorian post box on the corner that dates from 1856.

Cross Church Street and walk through the churchyard, then bear left to Market Hill, a triangular market place where you will see the town sign featuring the castle and the mere. Cross to the far side by a row of black-and-white timbered houses and go left. When you reach a crooked half-timbered cottage, turn right through the archway on to a narrow passage, Queen's Head Alley, named after the pub that once stood here.

Follow this path round to the left and turn right along Fore Street. Turn right again along Riverside, noting the unusual town pump with its two spouts, one for the townspeople and the other for horse-drawn water carts. Keep right along the river bank, passing the post office, then cross Bridge Street and keep straight ahead on a path alongside a two-storey block of flats to return to the car park.

WHILE YOU'RE THERE

Saxtead Green Post Mill, 2.5 miles (4km) north-west of Framlingham, is the best preserved 18th-century windmill in Suffolk. It is open during the summer months for tours and you can climb up the stairs to watch the mill turn on its post to face the wind.

Charsfield – 'Akenfield' Then and Now

Read the classic book then walk the landscape around a village immortalised in literature.

DISTANCE 5 miles (8km)	**MINIMUM TIME** 2hrs	
ASCENT/GRADIENT 262ft (80m) ▲▲▲	**LEVEL OF DIFFICULTY** +++	
PATHS Field paths, farm tracks, meadows, lanes, 2 stiles		
LANDSCAPE Rolling countryside of arable farmland and orchards		
SUGGESTED MAP OS Explorer 212 Woodbridge & Saxmundham		
START/FINISH Grid reference: TM 254564		
DOG FRIENDLINESS On lead on farmland		
PARKING Charsfield village hall		
PUBLIC TOILETS None en route		

In 1969, the poet Ronald Blythe produced a book that has come to be seen as a classic account of English village life. In it he recorded the memories of a generation of farm workers and painted an affectionate portrait of a way of life that was disappearing fast. The book was called *Akenfield* and it was based on the village of Charsfield.

Country Life

Blythe claimed never to have heard of oral history, but that is what Akenfield is. The book comes alive with the voices of the villagers, from the wheelwright and the saddler, to the gravedigger and the district nurse. Farmers, schoolteachers, horsemen and thatchers all gave him interviews and the result is a fascinating collection of tales. We hear from the doctor, the priest and the union leader and the Chairman of the Women's Institute, the magistrate, the vet and the survivors of World War I.

A Typical Suffolk Village

In many ways Charsfield was, and still is, a typical Suffolk village. It is not particularly pretty – in fact, says Blythe, if it was ever threatened by Ipswich overspill it is doubtful whether any preservation society would bother to save it. It has a mix of old cottages and modern council housing. And yet, according to Blythe, with 'its tall church on the hillside, a pub selling local brew, a pretty stream, a football pitch, a school with jars of tadpoles in the window, three shops with doorbells...it is the kind of place in which an Englishman has always felt it is his right and duty to live'.

Even as Blythe wrote the book, Charsfield was changing. Mechanisation meant that the blackcurrants no longer had to be picked by hand. Incoming professionals were building new bungalows on the hillsides. Many of the older residents had never left the village except to fight in the war, and a trip to Ipswich or even Wickham Market was once a major event. Now there were people who travelled each day to Ipswich to work, and there was even one businessman who commuted to London. As you walk around the village today on a quiet weekday afternoon, you can be sure that the

CHARSFIELD

number has increased. The shops have gone and the fields are mostly empty of workers, though at least the pub and the school have survived.

Akenfield is a hymn to the Suffolk countryside and to a way of life that has been lost. Blythe does not romanticise rural poverty. We meet Davie, born in 1887, who cannot read and write and has lived alone in the same house since his parents died when he was ten years old. You would be unlikely to meet anyone like David is Charsfield today.

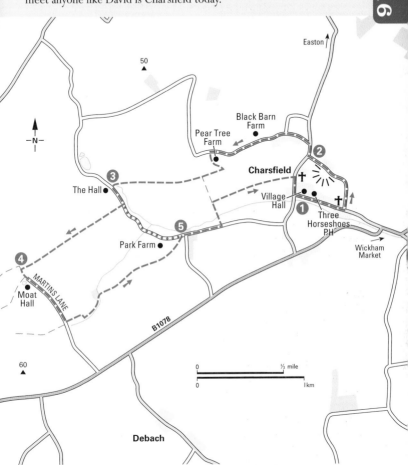

WALK 16 DIRECTIONS

1 Walk along The Street from the village hall, passing the Three Horseshoes pub. When you reach the Baptist chapel, turn left and walk up Chapel Lane. The road bends left and climbs to a summit. Your uphill walk is rewarded with good views over the village and the tower of St Peter's Church.

2 Turn right at the end of the lane. After 100yds (91m), turn left on to Magpie Street and stay on this lane for about 0.75 mile (1.2km) passing apple orchards on the left. Just after Pear Tree Farm, go left through the hedge on to an orchard-edge path. Keep to the left-hand side of the field and turn right on a grassy track that runs along the bottom of the orchard. Keep straight ahead on

W A L K 16

a paved track that passes between apple, pear and plum trees before descending to The Hall.

❸ Turn left along the road. For a short cut, you could stay on this road to reach Point ❺. For a longer walk, turn right in 150yds (137m) on to a cross-field path. At the far side of the field, keep straight ahead on a grassy track to climb towards a distant line of poplar trees, then continue ahead along the side of the next field.

❹ Turn left past an old barn and fork left by a pond to walk past Moat Hall Barn and along Martins Lane. After 600yds (549m), turn left across a meadow that runs behind a white house. The path turns right, bears left around a field, then turns sharply right as it approaches a line of trees. Go

straight through the trees, crossing a footbridge to reach a field with a huge oak tree at its centre. Turn right here along the edge of the field. In the corner of the field, take the overgrown path through the hedge. Cross the next field and go through a gate. Head for the right-hand corner at the bottom and go through another gate to reach a road.

❺ Turn right along the road, signposted 'Charsfield Street'. After 400yds (366m), turn left on to a wide track that climbs between fields. Turn right on to a surfaced track and stay on this across the fields, passing the small primary school before reaching St Peter's Church. Turn right and walk downhill to return to the start of the walk.

Down by the River at Woodbridge

A walk along the River Deben from a historic riverside town, with views of England's last working tide mill.

DISTANCE *4 miles (6.4km)*   MINIMUM TIME *1hr 30min*

ASCENT/GRADIENT *164ft (50m)* ▲▲▲   LEVEL OF DIFFICULTY +++

PATHS *River wall, riverside paths, town streets, some steps*

LANDSCAPE *Woodbridge and River Deben*

SUGGESTED MAP *OS Explorer 197 Ipswich, Felixstowe & Harwich or 212 Woodbridge & Saxmundham*

START/FINISH *Grid reference: TM 271485*

DOG FRIENDLINESS *Riverside paths suitable for dogs*

PARKING *The Avenue car park, Woodbridge*

PUBLIC TOILETS *On riverside near start of walk*

Woodbridge is one of those places that would have appealed to the water rat in Wind in the Willows, who declared that there was nothing, absolutely nothing, half so much worth doing as simply messing about in boats. Situated at the head of the Deben estuary, at the point where the river is navigable to the sea, Woodbridge attracts a sailing crowd who hang around its cafés and yacht club in summer, enthusiastically comparing mast sizes and discussing wind speeds like the people of Newmarket discuss horses and form.

Along the River Deben

This short walk takes you out along the River Deben among the sailing boats, marshes and mudflats. Seagulls swoop for fish and boats bob on the quayside, enhancing the nautical feel. On the way back you have the opportunity for a closer look at Woodbridge. The town owes much to Thomas Seckford, a courtier and legal adviser to Elizabeth I, who left the proceeds of his Clerkenwell Estate to Woodbridge. This generous bequest has been used to fund everything from hospitals to schools and playing fields and the Seckford Foundation continues to be administered for the benefit of the people of Woodbridge today. Seckford is buried in St Mary's Church, close to the abbey and the Shire Hall, which he built.

Tide Mill

There is also the chance to visit the Tide Mill, whose elegant white weatherboarded façade dominates the quay. A mill has stood on this site since at least the 12th century, although the present building dates from 1793 and was England's last working tide mill when it finally stopped turning in 1957. The mill was sold at auction in 1968, restored and opened to the public, and you can once again see the giant waterwheel turning at low tide. The old mill pond is now a marina, but a smaller pond has been dug to collect the water at high tide and release it when the tide has gone out. The times of the display, obviously, vary with the tides, but the wheel usually turns for an hour or so each day in summer, and if the tide is low enough you can see the channel created by the mill race as it flows back into the sea.

Kept Alive

Even if you struggle to understand the technology, this is still a fascinating example of Industrial Revolution machinery, kept alive by a team of dedicated volunteers. There are good views over the harbour and river from the upper floors.

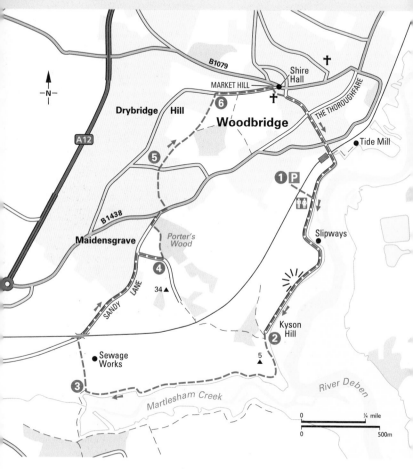

WALK 17 DIRECTIONS

❶ Leave the car park on The Avenue and cross the railway line to continue to the boatyard at the end of the lane. Turn right to walk along the river wall, passing the slipways of Deben Yacht Club. Continue along the river wall on an easy section of the walk, on a tarmac path with lovely views out over the meadows to your right, to enter the National Trust-owned land at Kyson Hill.

❷ Turn left at a three-way junction to drop down to the beach and continue the walk along the foreshore beneath a canopy of oak trees. (If the tide is high, you may

WOODBRIDGE

have to turn right instead, picking up the route at Point ❹.) Keep right at some wooden railings and follow this path round to Martlesham Creek, where you scramble up the embankment and follow a peaceful riverside path.

❸ Turn right at the end of the creek and walk around a sewage works to Sandy Lane. Turn right beneath the brick-arched railway bridge and stay on this road as it climbs steadily for about 700yds (640m). At the top of a rise, turn right on to Broom Heath.

❹ When the road bends round to the right, turn left past a gate leading to some Woodland Trust woods (Porter's Wood). (The short cut rejoins from the right here.) Stay on the path on the outside of the woods to return to Sandy Lane. Turn right here

and right again when you get to the main road, then cross the road and climb the steps on the far side after 50yds (46m). Keep straight ahead to the end of this footpath and cross a road to reach Portland Crescent.

❺ Keep straight ahead to drop down a hill and climb up the other side. Continue along Fen Walk, enclosed by black railings with graveyards to either side. Fork left at a junction of paths to drop down a grassy slope with views of the church tower up ahead. Keep straight ahead and climb the steps to Seckford Street.

❻ Turn right and stay on this road to reach Market Hill. An alleyway on the right-hand side leads you to the churchyard. Turn left through the churchyard on to Church Street, emerging alongside the site of the old abbey, now a private school. Walk down Church Street and cross over The Thoroughfare, an attractive pedestrian shopping street, on your left-hand side. Continue walking along Quay Street and cross the station yard to take the footbridge over the railway line. Once over, turn left to visit the Tide Mill or right to return to the start of the walk.

Overleaf: The Tide Mill and boats at Woodbridge (Walk 17)

A Warrior's Grave at Sutton Hoo

Mystery surrounds you on this atmospheric walk by the famous site of a pagan burial ground.

> **DISTANCE** 7.25 miles (11.7km) **MINIMUM TIME** 3hrs
>
> **ASCENT/GRADIENT** 262ft (80m) ▲▲▲ **LEVEL OF DIFFICULTY** ✦✦✦
>
> **PATHS** Field-edge and riverside paths, farm lanes, short section of busy road
>
> **LANDSCAPE** Farmland, woodland and River Deben
>
> **SUGGESTED MAP** OS Explorer 197 Ipswich, Felixstowe & Harwich
>
> **START/FINISH** Grid reference: TM 290493
>
> **DOG FRIENDLINESS** On lead on farmland and National Trust land
> (not allowed near burial mounds)
>
> **PARKING** National Trust car park – included in entry price for exhibition,
> or pay-and-display when exhibition closed (free to NT members)
>
> **PUBLIC TOILETS** At National Trust visitor centre – walkers' toilets behind
> building are open when visitor centre is closed

The discovery of an Anglo-Saxon ship burial at Sutton Hoo in 1939 shed new light on the Dark Ages and opened up a whole new chapter of English history. It all came about when Edith May Pretty, a widow with a keen interest in spiritualism, reported seeing visions of ghostly warriors dancing on the burial mounds near her home. She called in a local archaeologist, Basil Brown, to investigate and before long he had made his extraordinary discovery. Many of the graves had been desecrated by robbers but in one of the mounds he found the remains of a 90ft (27m) wooden ship with a burial chamber inside. The timber had rotted, leaving nothing but rusty iron rivets and a dark stain in the sand but the treasures that had survived included Byzantine silver, gold buckles and a bejewelled helmet, sword and shield. The only thing missing was a body, presumably decomposed.

Sutton Hoo Treasure

An inquest awarded the treasure to Mrs Pretty and she donated it to the British Museum, the single most generous gift ever received from a living donor. Archaeologists have been puzzling ever since over the identity of the missing man. Although weapon burials were not uncommon, the riches found at Sutton Hoo have led most experts to conclude that this was the burial ground of the early East Anglian kings, and that the burial chamber in the ship was that of King Raedwald, leader of the Wuffinga dynasty, who died around AD 625.

In 2002 the National Trust opened an exhibition on the site with replicas of many of the items and some of the original treasures on display. There is a sword in its wooden scabbard, the sword-belt fittings exquisitely patterned in gold and red garnet from India. There's an ornamental shield, covered in golden dragons and eagles, and a warrior's helmet with designs of horsemen in wrought copper and bronze. The artists making the replicas were full of admiration for the skills of their Anglo-Saxon ancestors. 'They were highly sophisticated people with an appreciation of art and culture. Some of these objects are extremely difficult to make even today,' says The National Trust.

Mystery Preserved

Most people agree that the new exhibition has made Sutton Hoo easier to understand. If, however, you prefer your lumps in the ground without any explanation, come here at dawn or on a misty morning in winter when the place still has an air of mystery about it and when you just might see ghostly figures dancing on the graves.

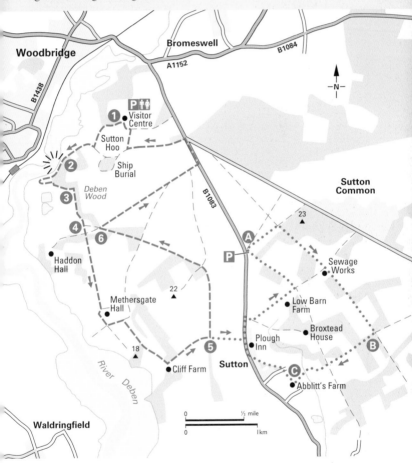

WALK 18 DIRECTIONS

❶ From the National Trust car park, take the signposted blue trail from behind the National Trust visitor centre, descending towards the River Deben on a gravel track. Turn left opposite the entrance

to Little Haugh and turn right by a map of the Sutton Hoo Estate. The path narrows and turns left alongside a fence on its way to the river. Keep left around a meadow and climb the steps to the river bank with Woodbridge visible on the opposite bank.

2 Turn left and walk along the river bank. The path is overgrown in places and the plank bridges can be slippery in wet weather but the views are superb. After 400yds (366m), climb the steps to your left to leave the river behind and turn left around a turf field. Keep to the edge of the field as it swings right and climbs between woodland to the left and a reservoir to the right.

WHILE YOU'RE THERE

It would be a pity not to visit the National Trust exhibition and treasury, which contains some of the original finds from Sutton Hoo. It is open daily in summer and on winter weekends, though times may vary throughout the year. From here, a specially signed pathway leads around the burial grounds. At weekends and during the summer holidays, members of the Sutton Hoo Society give fascinating guided tours of the site with the opportunity to climb on the burial mounds.

WHERE TO EAT AND DRINK

The only option on this walk is the restaurant at the National Trust visitor centre at Sutton Hoo. It is open daily in the summer and on winter weekends, offering a menu of soups, salads, sandwiches, local sausages, 'Anglo-Saxon' bread, tea and cakes. The Plough Inn at Sutton village is situated on the route of Walk 19.

beside a brick wall. You pass a pair of cannon on the lawn of the hall and continue ahead with the River Deben opening out in front of you. Go through a gate and turn left across a field then go through another gate and turn right along a lane. Stay on this lane for 1 mile (1.6km) and as it bends left past Cliff Farm.

3 Turn right at the top of a rise to follow a bridleway along the field-edge with Deben Wood to your left. At the end of the wood, the path swings half left across a field, then passes through a hedge on to a lane. You could turn left here for a short cut, picking up the walk again in 300yds (274m) at Point **6**.

5 At the second three-finger signpost turn left along a field-edge track, passing an embankment on the right. Keep to the public bridleway as it swings left around an area of woodland. At the end of the woodland, keep straight ahead between fields and continue as the path becomes a broad grass track through trees, passing some cottages to reach a minor lane.

4 Keep straight ahead for 0.75 mile (1.2km), crossing the drive to Haddon Hall. At Methersgate Hall bear right around farm buildings, then left on a footpath

6 Turn right and stay on this lane for about 1 mile (1.6km) to the main road (B1083). Turn left and walk carefully along the verge for 400yds (366m), soon to take the footpath left opposite the road junction. When you see the burial mounds to your left-hand side, turn right to return to the visitor centre on a National Trust permissive path.

WHAT TO LOOK OUT FOR

If you think some of the fields around here look like the pristine fairways of golf courses, you would be right. Turf is grown at Sutton Hoo especially for sports pitches, and exported to golf courses and cricket grounds in much drier countries such as Saudi Arabia.

Sutton Heath Sandlings

A loop across the heathland that once covered this part of Suffolk.
See map and information panel for Walk 18

DISTANCE 4.5 miles (7.2km)	MINIMUM TIME 2hrs
ASCENT/GRADIENT 98ft (30m) ▲▲▲	LEVEL OF DIFFICULTY +++

WALK 19 DIRECTIONS
(Walk 18 option)

Sutton Heath is part of the Sandlings, an area of lowland heath that once covered much of east Suffolk but most of which has been lost in the last two centuries to forestry, farming and urban development. This walk takes you across open heathland carpeted with heather and gorse, where you might be lucky enough to see rabbits, fallow deer or even adders.

At Point **5**, instead of turning left, keep straight ahead for 500yds (457m) to reach a road. Turn left along the road for 200yds (183m) then turn right on to a byway leading to Broxtead House. After 100yds (91m), turn left on a concrete track that becomes a sandy lane after passing Low Barn Farm. Turn left at a crossroads and stay on this path across the heathland of heather and bracken to reach a car park, Point **A**.

Cross the car park to the right and take the path through the gate, marked 'S1'. Follow this path as it bears slightly right across the heath to enter the trees. Turn right on to a crossing track and keep straight ahead through the woods to emerge at a clearing. Continue ahead with a field on

your left, following the sandy track down and uphill and keep straight ahead at a sewage works. Continue ahead for another 0.75 mile (1.2km), passing through a gate and taking a farm track between fields.

Turn right at a crossroads of paths, Point **B**, on a sandy lane that passes between tall Scots pines. Stay on this path and keep straight ahead when it is crossed by another wide sandy track. The path bends right and left to cross a stream and becomes a concrete lane. To either side of the lane is land that is managed under a countryside stewardship scheme, to which walkers have free access.

When the lane bends left at a group of farm cottages, Point **C**, turn right to pass Abblitt's Farm. Keep straight ahead at a junction by bungalows and turn left on a field-edge path that follows the line of the hedge to meet a road at Sutton village. Turn right and stay on the pavement past the Plough Inn. Cross the road just beyond the village sign and turn left through the gates to return to Point **5**.

Maritime Ipswich

*Explore the best of Ipswich old and new
on this easy stroll down to the docks.*

WALK 20

DISTANCE 2 miles (3.2km)	MINIMUM TIME 1hr
ASCENT/GRADIENT Negligible ▲▲▲	LEVEL OF DIFFICULTY ✚✚✚
PATHS Town streets, lanes and dockside promenade	
LANDSCAPE Ipswich town and its port	
SUGGESTED MAP Ipswich street map from tourist information centre	
START/FINISH Grid reference: TM 162446	
DOG FRIENDLINESS Not very suitable	
PARKING Town centre car parks, or Park-and-Ride car parks off A14	
PUBLIC TOILETS Buttermarket shopping centre	

WALK 20 DIRECTIONS

The county town of Ipswich makes for a pleasant day out and there is easy walking along the pedestrianised streets of the historic centre. Founded as the Anglo-Saxon trading port of Gipeswic around AD 600, it retains much of its original street plan. A dozen medieval churches survive in the town centre, surrounded by modern offices and shops. There are half-timbered houses and inns and the remains of a medieval priory, but also one of the most spectacular modern buildings in Suffolk.

This short walk begins in the town centre and works its way down to the docks, built in the 19th century on the site of the original Saxon shore. Start at Cornhill, the focal point of Ipswich and the historic setting for markets, fairs and executions. In 1555, the so-called Ipswich Martyrs were burned at the stake here for their Protestant beliefs. The square is dominated by the Town Hall, erected in 1868 and crowned by female figures representing Commerce,

Justice, Learning and Agriculture. The old post office, now a bank, is also Victorian and has more female figures depicting Industry, Electricity, Steam and Commerce.

With the post office behind you, turn right to walk along Tavern Street, once filled with pubs but now a pedestrian shopping street. On your right you pass The Walk, a mock-Tudor shopping arcade built in 1933. Turn right along Dial Lane, passing St Lawrence's Church. At the crossroads with Buttermarket, note the Ancient House opposite, with its carved woodwork and decorative pargeting.

Keep ahead into Arras Square, passing between St Stephen's Church, now the tourist information centre, and the Buttermarket shopping centre. At the end, turn left along Dogs Head Street and right at the crossroads along Lower Brook Street. Turn left along Rosemary Lane between the red-brick Peninsular House, offices of the P&O shipping company, and Haven House, home to Customs and Excise. Continue around a multi-storey car park to emerge opposite some almshouses. Turn left here and then right along an alleyway beside the ruins of 13th-century Blackfriars Priory, set in the gardens of a block of flats.

Cross Lower Orwell Street by a timber-framed cottage and turn right along Fore Street. Cross Star Lane via the pedestrian crossing and walk past the Fore Street Baths. At the next junction, fork left past the half-timbered Lord Nelson pub and continue along Fore Street. Cross the road and turn right beside the new University building to reach the Wet Dock, the largest in England when it opened in 1842.

WHERE TO EAT AND DRINK

A 17th-century dockside pub has been turned into Cobbold's On The Quay, where you can enjoy lunch overlooking the marina. The Lord Nelson on Fore Street serves ales from the cask and good traditional pub food. The Golden Lion and Manning's are two medieval inns on Cornhill with tables out on the square.

In common with dockland areas in other English cities, the Wet Dock is in the process of gentrification and now houses a mixture of wharves, warehouses, apartments, yachts and waterside pubs. Turn right to walk along Neptune Quay, passing old maltings and dockside inns. After walking beneath the modern glass

WHAT TO LOOK OUT FOR

On the corner of Princes Street and Queen Street, close to the end of the walk, is a sculpture of a large woman with a handbag and an umbrella. This is Grandma, the best-known character of the cartoonist Carl Giles (1916–95), who lived in Ipswich and worked in the office across the road.

WHILE YOU'RE THERE

The Ipswich Museum on High Street contains a full-size reproduction of a woolly mammoth, based on a skeleton discovered in Suffolk. Also on display in the natural history gallery are a giraffe, a rhino and a group of gorillas, all mounted in their original Victorian cases.

extension to Waterfront House, a 19th-century warehouse, you come to the Old Custom House where you can climb to the terrace for the best view of the docks. Continue along the quayside to the end of the dock, then turn right along Foundry Lane and left along College Street past the gateway of a 16th-century college founded by Cardinal Thomas Wolsey.

Turn right beside St Peter's Church and continue up St Peter's Street, which soon becomes St Nicholas' Street. On the corner of Silent Street, note the fine timber-framed house with a plaque to Thomas Wolsey (1475–1530), the son of an Ipswich butcher who became Lord Chancellor of England under Henry VIII but was eventually charged with high treason. Two doors along, another plaque marks the birthplace of the author VS Pritchett (1900–97).

Turn left down a pair of steps along a narrow passage leading to the Unitarian meeting house (1699), one of the first Nonconformist chapels in England. Walk round to the right of the church to reach the Willis-Corroon building, a remarkable black glass structure designed by Sir Norman (now Lord) Foster in 1975. Cross the road and turn left, then right along Princes Street to return to Cornhill, the start of the walk.

Constable Country at Flatford Mill

A walk through the landscape that inspired one of England's greatest artists.

WALK 21

DISTANCE 3.75 miles (6km)   MINIMUM TIME 1hr 30min

ASCENT/GRADIENT 246ft (75m) ▲▲▲   LEVEL OF DIFFICULTY +++

PATHS Roads, field paths and riverside meadows, 7 stiles

LANDSCAPE Pastoral landscapes of Stour Valley

SUGGESTED MAP OS Explorer 196 Sudbury, Hadleigh & Dedham Vale

START/FINISH Grid reference: TM 069346

DOG FRIENDLINESS Dogs should be kept mostly on lead

PARKING Free car park next to Red Lion, East Bergholt

PUBLIC TOILETS In car park and at Flatford visitor information centre

---

John Constable (1776–1837), the greatest English landscape painter of all time, was born in East Bergholt and spent his childhood among the leafy lanes and pastoral landscapes of Dedham Vale. Even after he moved to London to join the Royal Academy, he returned to Suffolk each summer to draw fresh inspiration from the bucolic scenery of meadows, valleys, rivers, farmland and boats. He claimed to have seen pictures in these scenes long before he ever picked up a pencil and they remained his favourite subject throughout his life. 'I associate my careless boyhood with all that lies on the banks of the Stour. Those scenes made me a painter and I am grateful,' he wrote.

Pastoral Landscapes

This walk takes you through the heart of Constable Country, which looks remarkably as it did when he painted it. Artists can still be seen with sketchbooks in hand, painting in the open air as Constable used to do. Several of his best-known works were painted in the vicinity of Flatford Mill, a watermill once owned by Golding Constable, the artist's father. The mill itself is now an environmental studies centre but you can stand outside and gaze across the mill pond at Willy Lott's House, familiar to art lovers around the world from its appearance in *The Hay Wain*. Willy Lott was a local farmer who lived in this house for 84 years and is said never to have travelled further than the churchyard of East Bergholt, where he is buried. Constable saw his friend Willy Lott as a symbol of the stability of the English countryside and this painting, more than any other, has come to represent the essence of rural England. It is on display in the National Gallery in London.

East Bergholt

The walk passes a number of sights associated with John Constable. His childhood home, East Bergholt House, is no longer there but a plaque on the railings marks the spot. His first studio is near by. On Fen Lane you walk along the route which Constable took on his way to school in Dedham each morning. Best of all, you get to stand in the places where Constable produced some of his finest paintings, such as *The Cornfield*, *The White Horse* and *Boat Building at Flatford Mill*. If you want to know more, the National Trust organises one-hour guided walks from Bridge Cottage in summer, where you visit the scenes of the paintings in the company of an art expert. Constable Country has become a popular place to visit and it can get crowded on summer weekends. If you can, come during the week or out of season, when the landscapes take on a completely different hue.

WALK 21

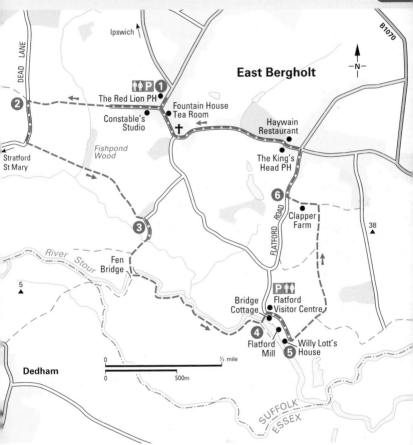

WALK 21 DIRECTIONS

1 Turn right out of the car park, pass the Red Lion pub and the post office, then turn right along a lane, noting Constable's early studio on the left. Continue along this lane, past a chapel and a cemetery, through a gate and down the left side of a meadow to cross a footbridge. Climb the path on the far side for marvellous

views of the Stour Valley and the church towers at Dedham and Stratford St Mary.

2 Turn left at a junction of paths to walk down Dead Lane, a sunken footpath. At the foot of the hill, turn left on to a field-edge path. The path goes right then left to cross a stile on the edge of Fishpond Wood. Walk beside the wood for a few paces, then climb

EAST BERGHOLT

WALK 21

another stile into a field and walk beside the hedge to your right. The path switches to the other side of the hedge and back again before bending left around a belt of woodland to Fen Lane.

❸ Turn right along the lane, crossing a cart bridge and ignoring footpaths to the left and to the right as you continue towards the wooden-arched Fen Bridge. Cross the bridge and turn left to walk beside the River Stour towards Flatford on the wide open pasture of the flood plain.

WHILE YOU'RE THERE

Bridge Cottage at Flatford is a 16th-century thatched cottage owned by the National Trust, with a free exhibition on Constable and his paintings. The Granary, along the road to Flatford Mill, is a black-timbered, thatched farmhouse with a museum of rural bygones and rowing boats for hire on the river.

❹ Cross a bridge to return to the north bank of the river beside Bridge Cottage. Turn right here, passing a restored dry dock on the way to Flatford Mill.

❺ Walk past Willy Lott's House and turn left past the car park. An optional loop here, on a National Trust permissive path, leads right around the outside of Gibbonsgate Field beside a hedge. Otherwise, keep left on a wide track and go through the gate to join another National Trust path through Miller's Field. Stay on this path as it swings left and climbs to the top of the field, then go straight ahead through a kissing gate. Keep ahead, ignore the stile on the left and soon follow a fenced path to a T-junction of footpaths. Turn left here along the track to the rear of barns and continue down the

WHAT TO LOOK OUT FOR

Don't miss the medieval bell cage in the churchyard at East Bergholt, erected in 1531. The church bells here are some of the heaviest in England, weighing approximately 4.25 tons. The oldest dates back to 1450. The bells are still rung by hand on Sunday mornings. Near by, in a corner of the churchyard, is the tomb of John Constable's parents, Golding and Ann Constable.

drive of Clapper Farm to reach Flatford Road.

❻ Turn right along the road. At the crossroads, turn left passing the King's Head pub and Haywain Restaurant on the way back to East Bergholt. Stay on the pavement on the right side of the road to walk through the churchyard and return to the start of the walk.

WHERE TO EAT AND DRINK

The Red Lion, at the start of the walk, offers typical pub fare including daily vegetarian specials. Alternatively, you can enjoy morning coffee, light lunches or afternoon tea in the Fountain House Tea Room across the road. The National Trust tea rooms at Bridge Cottage serves light lunches and snacks. Near the end of the walk is the King's Head in the Burnt Oak district of East Bergholt.

Between Two Rivers

*Views of Harwich and Felixstowe from a lonely spit
between the Stour and Orwell estuaries.*

DISTANCE 6 miles (9.7km)   MINIMUM TIME 3hrs

ASCENT/GRADIENT 262ft (80m) ▲▲▲   LEVEL OF DIFFICULTY ✦✦✦

PATHS Field and riverside paths, country lanes, 2 stiles

LANDSCAPE Farmland between Stour and Orwell estuaries

SUGGESTED MAP OS Explorer 197 Ipswich, Felixstowe & Harwich

START/FINISH Grid reference: TM 246336

DOG FRIENDLINESS On lead on farmland, off lead on riverside path

PARKING Opposite Bristol Arms at Shotley Gate

PUBLIC TOILETS None en route

The rows of silent headstones in the sloping cemetery of St Mary's Church tell the story of HMS *Ganges*. Between 1905 and 1976, more than 150,000 recruits passed through the doors of this naval training establishment at Shotley. When they arrived, they were little more than boys, and some of them never came out. Among the graves of submariners killed in action and German prisoners of war are those of numerous boys aged from 15 to 17 who died before they ever got the chance to serve their country.

Training Centre

A newer churchyard across the way contains the graves of those killed in World War Two. Here are commanders, petty officers, ordinary seamen and 'a sailor of the 1939–45 war known unto God', the different ranks, named and unnamed, brought together in death. Here, too, are 16 crew members of HMS *Worcester*, who lost their lives in February 1942. And, from a later generation, a 19-year-old seaman who drowned in Nova Scotia in 1968. The first HMS *Ganges* was built in 1782, a gift to the Royal Navy from the East India Company. A second ship of the same name was manufactured at the Bombay shipyards and eventually became a boys' training ship, arriving at Shotley in 1899. The ship left but HMS *Ganges* remained, as the name of a new shore-based training centre. Discipline was legendary. Edward, Prince of Wales, said in the 1930s that it made the French Foreign Legion seem like a Sunday school. This was a regime of cold showers and rations of bread and cheese, a system designed to take boys and turn them into men.

Change of Use

HMS *Ganges* will soon be developed for housing, though the 142ft (43m) tall mast that stands in the parade ground will remain as a memorial to its past. At one time it was the custom for naval cadets to shin up the mast during training. In 1918, to celebrate the end of World War One, the entire school of boys climbed the mast, resulting in several accidents.

Shotley is situated on a lonely peninsula where the rivers Stour and Orwell meet as they flow into the sea. To one side is the ferry port at Harwich, to

SHOTLEY

the other Felixstowe Docks. The area has historical associations with Anne Boleyn (1501–36), the second wife of Henry VIII and mother of Elizabeth I, and whose uncle was the owner of Erwarton Hall. Before her execution, she is said to have requested that her heart be buried at Erwarton. There is no evidence that it happened, but in 1836 a lead casket in the shape of a heart was found in a wall of the church. It is now buried beneath the organ.

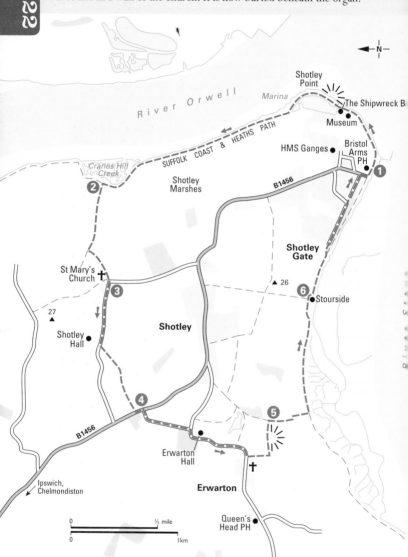

WALK 22 DIRECTIONS

❶ Start at the Bristol Arms, looking across to Harwich, and head left along the waterfront to Shotley Marina. Pass to the right

of the HMS *Ganges* Museum (open on summer weekends) and keep right to walk across the lock gates to Shotley Point. A path follows the headland around the marina basin, with good views of Felixstowe

Docks. Turn right to continue along the flood bank between marshes and mudflats. After 1 mile (1.6km) the path passes some old oyster beds and swings left beside the salt marshes at Crane's Hill Creek.

2 Half-way around the creek, where you see a three-finger signpost, descend the bank to your left and cross a stile to join a meadow-edge path. Cross a stile and bear left along a track to climb past vineyards to St Mary's Church.

WHILE YOU'RE THERE

Pin Mill, near the village of Chelmondiston, is a popular sailing centre with Thames barges moored on the quayside by the 17th-century Butt and Oyster pub. The National Trust owns a stretch of woodland here overlooking the Orwell Estuary, and a circular walk of 1.5 miles (2.4km) leads on to the cliff and back along the foreshore.

---

3 Walk straight ahead at the crossroads beyond the church, on a tarmac lane leading to Shotley Hall, then turn left on to a cross-field path opposite the drive. Follow this path diagonally across the field, then bear right at the far corner, following the line of telegraph poles towards a road where you turn left.

4 After 50yds (46m), turn right along a lane, signposted 'Erwarton Walk'. At the end of this lane, turn right, passing the red-brick Tudor gatehouse of Erwarton Hall. Stay on this quiet country road as it bends towards Erwarton village. Just after a right-hand bend, turn left beside the churchyard on to a wide track. Pass to the right of a cottage and turn left along a field-edge path with fine views over the River Stour.

WHAT TO LOOK OUT FOR

The Shotley Marshes beside the River Orwell are home to a number of wading birds. Among those to look out for are redshank (speckled brown body, red beak and bright red legs), lapwing (black and white with a pointed crest) and snipe (with its distinctive long, straight bill). In spring you may also spot nesting coots, moorhens and tufted ducks

---

5 At the end of the field, turn right and follow the field-edge down to the River Stour. Turn left and follow the Suffolk Coast and Heath Path beside the river, eventually passing a row of cottages and a property called Stourside.

WHERE TO EAT AND DRINK

The Bristol Arms at Shotley Gate specialises in fresh fish and the Shipwreck Bar at Shotley Marina is open all day for tea, coffee, home-made cakes and a wide range of bar meals. If you want to break your walk, a good alternative is the Queen's Head at Erwarton, a traditional country pub not far from the route of the walk.

---

6 Continue between fields and the river and soon climb gently through trees to houses and a road. Follow the road and keep straight on along a tarmac path where the road curves left. Join another road and follow this to a T-junction. Turn right downhill back to The Bristol Arms on the left.

Fish and Ships by the Felixstowe Ferry

*See another side to this busy coastal resort
on a pleasant walk along the Deben Estuary.*

DISTANCE 6.5 miles (10.4km) **MINIMUM TIME** 3hrs

ASCENT/GRADIENT 164ft (50m) ▲▲▲ **LEVEL OF DIFFICULTY** ✦✦✦

PATHS Field and riverside paths, country lanes, farm tracks, sea wall, 4 stiles

LANDSCAPE Farmland, estuary and coast

SUGGESTED MAP OS Explorer 197 Ipswich, Felixstowe & Harwich

START/FINISH Grid reference: TM 328376

DOG FRIENDLINESS Mostly off lead except across farmland

PARKING Ferry Café car park (fee), Felixstowe Ferry

PUBLIC TOILETS At Felixstowe Ferry

Felixstowe, whose name means 'happy place', is a large Edwardian seaside resort that continues to provide thousands of families with buckets of summer fun. The English beach holiday may be in terminal decline thanks to cheap flights to the Mediterranean, but Felixstowe still embodies the carefree, kiss-me-quick atmosphere of an earlier age. Children ride bumper boats, go fishing for crabs and buy sticks of rock from kiosks on the pier. Pensioners stroll along the promenade and drink tea at seafront cafés. At the same time, Felixstowe has grown to become Britain's largest container port, as you will discover if you take Walk 25.

Fishing Huts and Ferry

This walk shows you another side of Felixstowe, well away from the arcades and the sandcastles on the beach. It starts in the small hamlet of Felixstowe Ferry, with its boatyard, fishing huts and ferry across the river. The café here serves some of the freshest fish and chips you will find, but if that is still not fresh enough you can buy fish straight off the fishing boat at the huts down by the quay.

The walk leads along the estuary of the River Deben and beside the King's Fleet, a peaceful stream that takes its name from the fleet of ships assembled here by Edward III ready to sail to France. The King's Fleet is no longer navigable but back in the 13th century it was regularly used by trading ships.

Martello Towers

Returning to the sea, you pass two Martello towers, rare survivors of a chain of defensive outposts built between 1805 and 1812 to protect the English coastline against a threatened invasion by Napoleon of France. These round towers were 30ft (9m) tall and had walls up to 13ft (4m) thick in order to withstand incoming cannonballs. Ironically, they were based on a tower at Mortella Point in Corsica, Napoleon's birthplace, which the British Navy had tried unsuccessfully to bombard. The towers were three storeys high and contained living quarters for one officer and 24 men, together with gunpowder stores, provisions and a gun tower on the roof.

FELIXSTOWE FERRY

Line of Follies

By 1815 Napoleon had been defeated at Waterloo and the Martello towers were redundant. The promised invasion never took place and none of the towers ever fired a shot in anger. Many of them have disappeared without trace into the sea, but a few of the towers remain, such as a line of follies decorating the East Anglian coast. One of the towers at Felixstowe was used for some time by the coastguard, and another at Felixstowe Ferry is now a private house. They stand above the beach as lonely reminders of the time when England faced the real threat of foreign invasion.

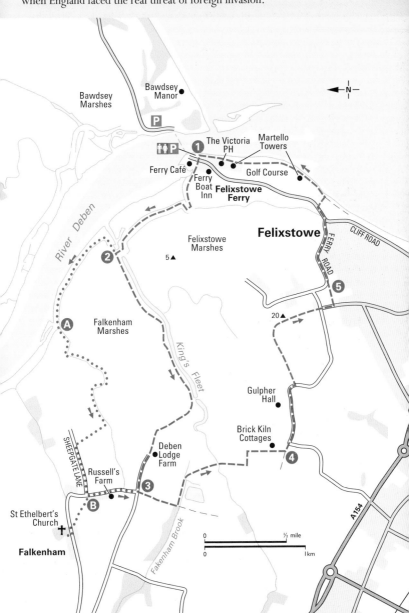

WALK 23 DIRECTIONS

1 Take the tarmac path along an embankment behind the Ferry Café car park. The path passes the boatyard and follows the river wall as you look down on abandoned boats lying moored in muddy flats. Turn right through a squeeze stile to walk beside the Deben Estuary. After 0.5 mile (800m) the path swings left and then right across an inlet at the entrance to King's Fleet.

WHERE TO EAT AND DRINK

The Ferry Café is little more than a beach hut but it has established a dedicated following for its fish and chips and all-day breakfasts. There are also two popular pubs at Felixstowe Ferry, the Victoria and the Ferry Boat Inn.

2 Turn left to descend the embankment and walk along a broad track. You pass an old wind pump and stay on this track as it winds its way between farmland and King's Fleet. After 1 mile (1.6km) the track bends right and climbs to a farm where it becomes a tarmac lane. Continue until you reach a T-junction.

3 Turn left across the field to climb to a ridge then drop down through the next field to The Wilderness, a belt of trees beside Falkenham Brook. Turn left through the trees

WHILE YOU'RE THERE

Spend some time in Felixstowe, with its beaches, pier, amusement arcades, promenade, seafront gardens, crazy golf and Punch and Judy shows. The kids will love it and adults can enjoy some gentle nostalgia. Another fun thing to do in summer is to take the foot ferry across the river from Felixstowe Ferry to Bawdsey and back again.

and follow this path alongside the stream, then bend right to cross a stile and a meadow. Make for the corner of a hedge opposite and bear right alongside a fence to cross a footbridge and continue on a grassy path between the fields. When you get to the end of a field, turn left and continue to the end of a hedge, then turn right to climb a track to Brick Kiln Cottages.

WHAT TO LOOK OUT FOR

As you walk back along the sea wall, look across the river to see Bawdsey Manor, a Victorian pile built by Sir Cuthbert Quilter in 1886. The manor was taken over by the government in the 1930s and it was here that Sir Robert Watson-Watt (1892–1973) perfected the science of radar following his early experiments on Orford Ness (see Walk 10). A radar mast can still be seen above the trees.

4 At the top of the track, turn left along a lane and stay on this lane past Gulpher Hall and its duck pond. As the road bends right, walk past the entrance to The Brook and turn left on a field-edge path. The path ascends then turns right around a field and cuts straight across the field corner, unless it's diverted by crops. Pass through a gate and keep straight on along the lane, then turn left before houses in 150yds (137m) to join another path that runs between fields.

5 When you reach a pill box, turn right on to Ferry Road. Cross Cliff Road and turn left, walking past the clubhouse and turning half right across the golf course on a signposted path to reach the sea wall. Turn left and walk along the wall, passing two Martello towers and a row of beach huts. Continue to the mouth of the estuary and turn left just before the jetty to return to the Ferry Café.

Across Falkenham Marshes

A longer walk across an area of reclaimed marshland to a peaceful church.

See map and information panel for Walk 23

DISTANCE 7.75 miles (12.5km) (includes detour to Falkenham church)	
MINIMUM TIME 3hrs 30min	
ASCENT/GRADIENT 230ft (70m) ▲▲▲	**LEVEL OF DIFFICULTY** +++
PATHS 5 stiles	

WALK 24 DIRECTIONS (Walk 23 option)

Turn right at Point **2** and continue along the estuary instead of taking the path to King's Fleet. Stay on the river embankment for about 0.75 mile (1.2km). When you can see the marina at Ramsholt coming into view in the distance on the opposite bank, cross a stile to turn left across Falkenham Marshes, Point **A**.

Drop steeply down the bank on to a grassy path and follow this path alongside a ditch. The path crosses a lovely area of marshland that has been mostly reclaimed for agriculture, with ditches such as this draining the water that would otherwise flood the land. Cross a footbridge to the far side of the ditch to join a narrow field-edge path, then cross back over another footbridge. Eventually the path swings sharply to the right and climbs to a road, Sheepgate Lane.

Turn left here and walk for 500yds (457m) to reach a junction, Point **B**. At this point it is worth making a short detour by taking the cross-field path opposite that leads diagonally towards the village of Falkenham and St Ethelbert's Church. The church is

dedicated to an 8th-century Saxon King of East Anglia and is set in its own wooded gardens, with fine views over the marshes and the river. You may also be able to spot All Saints Church at Ramsholt across the river, easily identified by its Saxon round tower.

Back to St Ethelbert's – the 15th-century tower of flint and stone is typical of Suffolk churches. Beneath the tower, the west doorway features the royal coats of arms of England and France. If the church is open, take the opportunity to go inside and admire its fine hammerbeam roof and the beautifully carved font, whose angels managed to survive the attention of the zealous 17th-century Puritans when the villagers plastered them over to prevent them being smashed to pieces as 'superstitious images'. The carvings were only rediscovered in Victorian times.

Return to Point **B** and turn right along the road (if you have not taken the diversion to the church, turn left instead). The road descends past Russell's Farm with distant views of the coast then climbs gently to reach Point **3** on the route of Walk 23.

Lonely Landguard Point

*A wild walk to the very edge of Suffolk,
with views over Felixstowe docks.*

DISTANCE 2 miles (3.2km)	MINIMUM TIME 1hr

ASCENT/GRADIENT *Negligible* ▲▲▲ LEVEL OF DIFFICULTY ✦✦✦

PATHS *Sand and shingle beach, grass, concrete lanes, some steps*

LANDSCAPE *Shingle, grassland, sea and docks*

SUGGESTED MAP *OS Explorer 197 Ipswich, Felixstowe & Harwich*

START/FINISH *Grid reference: TM 289325*

DOG FRIENDLINESS *Dogs must be kept on lead in Landguard Reserve*

PARKING *Manor Terrace car park (free), Felixstowe*

PUBLIC TOILETS *At car park*

WALK 25 DIRECTIONS

This is a walk for people who find beauty in bleak landscapes and charm in the most unexpected places. You won't find any meadows or fields of wheat, just a shingle beach and a lonely spit where Suffolk dips its toe into the sea. You won't see country cottages or half-timbered farmhouses, but you will see gantries and cranes. If you're looking for a rural ramble, don't say you weren't warned!

From the car park in Manor Terrace you can walk straight into Landguard Reserve, pausing to look at the interpretation board on the way. This small nature reserve contains at least one per

cent of all Britain's vegetated shingle, a delicate ecosystem that is constantly under threat. The shingle spit here has been formed by the action of the tides over millions of years and has been colonised by rare plants such as the seakale and yellow-horned poppy. At the same time there are also reminders of human presence in the form of earthworks and anti-invasion defences at this strategic spot at the mouth of the Orwell and Stour rivers.

Take the gravel path ahead of you to climb an embankment. Walk along the top of the bank for about 200yds (183m) then drop down some steps and climb up on the other side to a second embankment with good views of Felixstowe and its beach. The path drops down to a concrete track. After passing an information board, bear left across the grass and shingle towards the beach. In spring and summer, you will notice that parts of the beach have been roped off to prevent any disturbance to nesting birds. Little tern return here each spring after wintering in Africa and ringed

WHAT TO LOOK OUT FOR

The unpleasant stinking goosefoot, named after its smell of rotting fish, grows at only three sites in Britain and one of them is the Landguard Reserve. The plant flowers between July and October and its flowers are said to resemble miniature broccoli florets.

plover arrive from the nearby estuaries to lay their eggs in the shingle, cleverly camouflaged to resemble pebbles.

Walk right along the beach towards the jetty at Landguard Point. This is Suffolk's southernmost point, a wild and windswept place where fishermen can sometimes be seen casting their rods into the sea. Beneath the groyne there are views of Harwich across the river. Turn right and walk away from the jetty beside a fenced-off area, following the fence round to the left past a group of concrete blocks. After passing a red house, bear slightly right and continue beside another fenced-off area. Behind the fence is the Bird Observatory, where 8,000 birds are trapped, ringed and released each year in an effort to understand migratory patterns and population trends. A board outside the observatory lists recent sightings and describes the annual migrations of birds like wood pigeon who travel south to Africa in winter and brent geese who arrive from Siberia to benefit from the warmer climes that the pigeons are leaving behind.

Turn left at the end of the fence to leave the nature reserve through a gate. On your left is Landguard Fort, begun in the 18th century but with recent additions up to 1950. It was from an earlier fortress on this site that one of the last attempted invasions of England, by the Dutch fleet in 1667, was repelled. Walk around the fort to the right and you will come to

the John Bradfield viewing area overlooking Felixstowe Docks. On most days you will find a surprising number of people here, admiring the ferries and cruise ships and watching the dockers at work bringing shiploads of containers ashore. This is the largest container port in England, the fourth largest in Europe and the thirteenth largest in the world. The statistics are staggering. At its two terminals, the Port of Felixstowe operates 20 ship-to-shore cranes and manages to deal with more than two million containers each year. In contrast to all these big ships, a foot ferry crosses the river from here to Shotley and Harwich in summer.

Return to the fort and continue straight ahead beside the road, passing some concrete defence structures to your right. At the end of the fence, bear right to return to the nature reserve. Climb the steps on the left to reach another embankment. Walk along this, then descend some steps and return across the left-hand side of the reserve with a caravan site in the distance and the shiny glass structure of Felixstowe customs house to your left.

Buildings of Kersey and Hadleigh

A lesson in Suffolk architecture on a cross-country walk from a pretty village to a historic town.

DISTANCE 7 miles (11.3km)   MINIMUM TIME 3hrs

ASCENT/GRADIENT 525ft (160m) ▲▲▲   LEVEL OF DIFFICULTY +++

PATHS Field paths, country roads, town streets, 1 stile

LANDSCAPE Undulating farmland between Kersey and Hadleigh

SUGGESTED MAP OS Explorer 196 Sudbury, Hadleigh & Dedham Vale

START/FINISH Grid reference: TM 001440

DOG FRIENDLINESS On lead across farmland

PARKING The Street, Kersey (between church and Splash)

PUBLIC TOILETS Off High Street, Hadleigh

The village of Kersey, nestling deep in its own small vale, is one of those places that captures the essence of rural Suffolk. Medieval houses and cottages line the main street, climbing up steep slopes to either side of a ford. Children throw bread to the ducks. A thatcher works on a roof. Come here on a summer day and it is such a perfect scene that it is easy to forget that most of the locals have gone off to work in Ipswich and that the people you see are tourists.

Medieval Houses

This walk takes you across the fields from Kersey to Hadleigh, a historic market town full of interesting buildings. From the 14th to 16th centuries, Hadleigh was a centre of the wool trade, and many of the half-timbered merchants' houses along the High Street date from that time. Timber-framing was common in East Anglia, using oak from coppiced woods, with large uprights used to build the main frame and the spaces between the timbers filled with 'wattle' (smaller sticks bundled together with twine) and 'daub' (a mixture of mud and straw) before being coated with whitewash or lime. Even those houses that appear to have Georgian brick façades are often timber-framed underneath.

Ornamental Plasterwork

Another common feature of Suffolk architecture, both here and in the other wool towns, is pargeting. This involves decorating the façade of a house with ornamental plasterwork, often in the form of symbols. There are several fine examples along Hadleigh High Street. Although pargeting is generally associated with the 17th century, there has recently been a revival of interest in this East Anglian craft and it is starting to appear on houses once again.

In the churchyard at Hadleigh are three contrasting buildings, each constructed from a different material. St Mary's Church, like most Suffolk churches, is built of flint, though unusually it has a spire rather than a tower. The 14th-century Guildhall is timber-framed and has been used as a market hall, workhouse, grammar school and corset factory before finding its present use as the town hall and council chamber. On summer afternoons you can enjoy a cream tea in the walled garden.

Oxford Movement

The red-brick Deanery Tower of 1495, six storeys high and surmounted by turrets, was built for William Pykenham, Archdeacon of Suffolk and rector of Hadleigh, as the gateway for a planned manor house. In 1833 it was the setting for one of the first meetings of the Oxford Movement, that aimed to restore traditional Catholic values and ritual to the Church of England. The three buildings together form a surprisingly harmonious ensemble, and the same could be said of Kersey and Hadleigh as a whole.

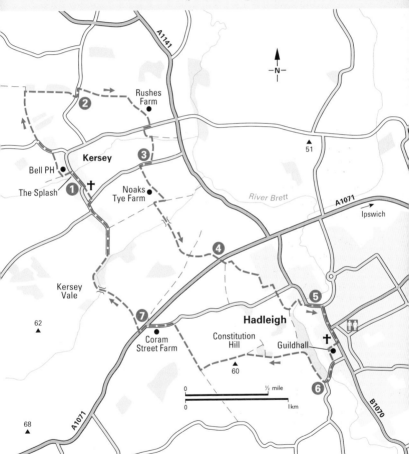

WALK 26 DIRECTIONS

❶ Walk down the main street and cross the Splash, the local name for the ford. After passing the first house, turn left along a track then right through the

allotments and climb a field-edge path to a road. Walk left for 150yds (137m) then turn right on a fenced-off path. At the end of the meadow, turn right beside a ditch, crossing a footbridge and arriving at a road.

KERSEY

WHAT TO LOOK OUT FOR

The pargeting above 99 High Street, Hadleigh, features the Tudor rose and the arms of Elizabeth I, as well as a golden lion.

2 Turn left and in 75yds (69m) go right on a bridleway between the trees. The path bends right and descends towards a farm. Turn right along the farm track and briefly right along a road, then left by a shed to cross a field. Turn left alongside a stream and cross a footbridge, then climb steps and continue uphill towards a road.

3 Turn right for 100yds (91m) then left on to a farm drive. Walk round to the left of the farm buildings and look for a narrow path alongside a hedge. When you reach a junction, turn right and go left before reaching a telegraph pole to cross the fields. Cross a footbridge and continue straight ahead before bearing half left to meet the A1071. This path may be diverted by crops so it is best to follow the obvious route rather than sticking to the right of way.

4 Cross the road, bear left across a field and turn left along a shady green lane. In a few paces bear half right across a field, keeping right at the field boundary, soon to follow the path between gardens to a road. Turn right, cross Friars Hill and walk past the cricket ground with the cemetery wall to your right. Pass through a gate

WHERE TO EAT AND DRINK

The Bell, beside the Splash in Kersey, is a medieval inn full of old-world character. There are plenty of options on Hadleigh High Street, including cafés, pubs and the George Inn, a historic coaching inn.

and turn left across the recreation ground to arrive at riverside meadows. Cross the footbridge and walk through the car park on to Bridge Street.

5 Turn right and right again to walk along High Street. After 400yds (366m), turn right along Church Street to reach St Mary's Church. The Guildhall is on your left. Walk through the gate to the right of the Guildhall (if this is closed, walk around the building to the left). Continue straight ahead to reach a road, then turn right to cross Toppesfield Bridge.

WHILE YOU'RE THERE

In summer, make sure to have tea in the gardens of Hadleigh Guildhall. The Guildhall is run by the Hadleigh Market Feoffment Charity, who also offer guided tours of the historic building.

6 Ignore the signposted Riverside Walk and turn to the right on a field-edge track behind the riverside park. When the path divides, keep left to climb to Broom Hill nature reserve and continue up Constitution Hill, ignoring paths left and right. Turn right at a wide track and continue to a road, where you turn left.

7 Turn left at the A1071, then right in a few paces on to a waymarked track. At the corner of a field, keep to the right to drop down towards a cottage. Cross a footbridge and stile to the right of the cottage and turn right along the lane to return to Kersey. Just after you pass a small green, follow the road round to the right and then turn left past the primary school to St Mary's Church. A steep footpath alongside the churchyard returns you to the main street.

Murder Most Foul at Polstead

On the trail of a grisly Victorian murder in the deceptively green valley of the River Box.

DISTANCE 4 miles (6.4km)   **MINIMUM TIME** 2hrs

ASCENT/GRADIENT 394ft (120m) ▲▲▲   **LEVEL OF DIFFICULTY** +++

PATHS Field-edge paths, meadows, country lanes, 4 stiles

LANDSCAPE Farmland, woodland, parkland and villages

SUGGESTED MAP OS Explorer 196 Sudbury, Hadleigh & Dedham Vale

START/FINISH Grid reference: TL 990381

DOG FRIENDLINESS Farmland – dogs on lead

PARKING Lay-by beside duck pond at Polstead

PUBLIC TOILETS None en route

A sensational murder in 1827 brought notoriety to the small Suffolk village of Polstead. With a young squire, a femme fatale and tales of dreams and disguise, the 'Murder in the Red Barn' had all the ingredients of a Victorian melodrama and it was soon appearing in 'penny dreadful' scandal sheets and popular plays.

Fatal Assignation

The two main characters were William Corder, the son of a tenant farmer, and Maria Marten, the pretty daughter of the village molecatcher, with whom he was having an affair. The 26-year-old Maria had already had two children by different lovers, one of whom, William's elder brother Thomas, had since drowned after falling through ice in the village pond. Maria and William would meet each night in the Red Barn, so called because of the way it glowed red in the setting sun. Eventually she became pregnant, though the baby only survived a few weeks and was buried secretly in a nearby field. Maria's parents demanded that William marry the girl, so he arranged for her to arrive at the barn disguised in man's clothing in order that they could elope to Ipswich out of sight of his disapproving parents and the village priest. Maria went to the barn for her assignation, but she never came out.

Grisly Discovery

William Corder moved to London, where he married a woman he had met through a 'lonely hearts' advertisement and set up a boarding school for girls. A year later, Maria's stepmother Anne dreamed that Maria had been murdered and buried in the Red Barn. Her body was discovered beneath the floorboards. She had been shot, stabbed and strangled for good measure. William was arrested and charged with her murder, and despite protesting his innocence, he was found guilty and hanged at Bury St Edmunds in August 1828.

The full story of the murder can be found in a booklet on sale at Polstead Community Shop. This walk passes close to several of the sites associated with the crime – though the barn itself is no longer there, it burned down in 1842. William Corder lived at Street Farm, the large farmhouse seen on the left as you descend to the duck pond from the village green. Brook Cottage, where Maria Marten was born, and Maria Marten's Cottage, where she later lived, can both be seen along Marten's Lane.

Maria's grave in the churchyard has been plundered by souvenir hunters but St Mary's Church is still worth a visit to see the 12th-century Norman stone spire and the brick arches in the chancel and nave, two features that make it unique among Suffolk churches.

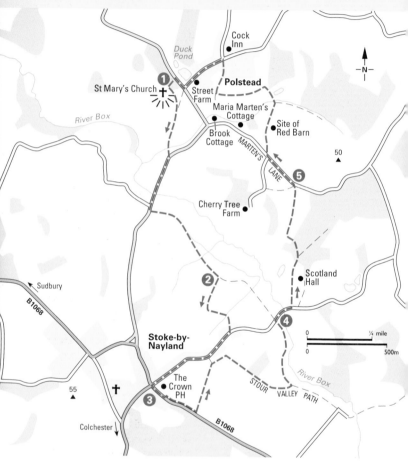

WALK 27 DIRECTIONS

❶ Walk up the lane opposite the duck pond towards St Mary's Church. From the churchyard there are views across the valley to Stoke-by-Nayland and its prominent church tower. Leave St Mary's churchyard through a gate on the left-hand side to enter

an area of pasture called The Horsecroft. Cross the meadow and bear right towards a white house. Pass the house, go through a gate and continue along the road for 0.25 mile (400m). After crossing a bridge, turn left over a stile, signed 'Scotland Street', on to a footpath that runs through a meadow.

2 Turn right at a junction of paths to enter the field to your left. The path climbs steadily around the edge of the field before turning right through a small wood to reach a road. Turn right and stay on this lane to walk into Stoke-by-Nayland. If you don't want to visit the village, take the short cut beside a house called Homestead on your left after about 200yds (183m).

WHAT TO LOOK OUT FOR

Polstead is known for a particular variety of cherry, the Polstead Black, which is made into a potent cherry brandy. A Cherry Fair used to be celebrated on the village green each July, and you can still see the cherries on sale at local farms and garden gates in summer.

WHERE TO EAT AND DRINK

The Cock Inn, on the village green at Polstead, serves good meals or you can pick up a snack at the Polstead Community Shop, situated in an annexe of the village hall. The Crown at Stoke-by-Nayland, at the mid-way point of the walk, offers imaginative pub food, good wines and East Anglian ales.

sharp left and walk along the field edge before crossing a stile to reach a road.

4 Turn right to cross the River Box, then turn left across a footbridge and pass through a kissing gate. Follow this path across meadows, with a marshy area to your left, to reach a kissing-gate and cross a footbridge. Turn immediately left, then keep ahead at a fork and gently climb to fork left through a gateway to enter a belt of woodland. Leaving the woods, turn right along a wide track that leads uphill to Marten's Lane.

3 Turn left at the crossroads and walk along the B1068, joining a permissive path alongside the road just beyond The Crown. Turn left through a gate when you see a Stour Valley Path waymark. The path descends alongside a tall hedge to meet up with the short cut, then follows the field-edge across undulating farmland and heads diagonally left across a field. At the far corner of the field, turn

5 Turn left along Marten's Lane. Just before the entrance to Cherry Tree Farm, turn right on to a footpath that skirts the edge of parkland to a stile and goes around a meadow to a stile on the right. This is the Red Barn Path that leads to the murder site. In a few paces, turn left through a kissing gate on the edge of the meadow, passing a small pond on the right. Stay on this enclosed path to pass through another kissing gate and cross a meadow where donkeys graze. Turn right when you get to the end of the meadow, climb to a kissing gate and walk between the houses to reach the village green. Turn left to walk downhill and return to the duck pond.

WHILE YOU'RE THERE

Although the walk skirts Stoke-by-Nayland, it is worth continuing into the village to visit St Mary's Church, whose 120ft (37m) brick and flint tower, featured in a painting by John Constable, dominates both the village and the surrounding area. Across the road is the 15th-century timber-framed Guildhall, once used as a workhouse but now converted into three cottages. Note also the former village lock-up on the edge of the churchyard.

In the Peaceful Gipping Valley

A walk in a tranquil valley,
looking out for herons, kingfishers and otters.

DISTANCE 5 miles (8km)   MINIMUM TIME 2hrs

ASCENT/GRADIENT 213ft (65m) ▲▲▲   LEVEL OF DIFFICULTY ✦✦✦

PATHS Riverside, field-edge and cross-field paths, 12 stiles

LANDSCAPE River, meadows and farmland

SUGGESTED MAP OS Explorer 211 Bury St Edmunds & Stowmarket

START/FINISH Grid reference: TM 123512

DOG FRIENDLINESS Mostly off lead, except where livestock grazing

PARKING Gipping Valley Centre

PUBLIC TOILETS At start of walk

The story of the Gipping Valley is of a river which has turned full circle, from peaceful rural backwater to industrial corridor and back again in the space of 200 years. Until the late 18th century, the Gipping between Stowmarket and Ipswich was a gently flowing river, popular with anglers. All that changed in 1790, when a team of 200 men spent three years working with picks and shovels, building locks and a tow path to turn the river into a canal. For the next hundred years, the Gipping was a hive of activity as mills, maltings and factories were built beside the river and barges travelled upstream as far as Stowmarket carrying timber, coal, bricks and malt.

Railway Ruin

The arrival of the railway brought a slow decline in river traffic and, by the early 20th century, th e Gipping was abandoned, its waters polluted by industrial waste. Just as rail replaced rivers, so roads replaced rail with the building of the A14 trunk road, carving through the heart of mid Suffolk on its way from Felixstowe to the Midlands. Much of the gravel used in its construction was quarried from the Gipping Valley, further scarring the landscape. Out of the ashes of destruction, however, has risen a new river whose waters are once again teeming with fish and whose reed beds provide habitats for wild flowers, butterflies and birds. Otters have even returned to the river.

The gravel pits have been flooded and turned into tranquil lakes, as popular with fishermen as they are with kingfishers and herons. This walk takes you along part of the Gipping Valley River Path, which runs for 17 miles (27km) from Stowmarket to Ipswich docks, where the Gipping becomes the River Orwell and continues its journey to the sea. You walk beside the river on the old tow path, passing woodland, lakes and wildflower meadows in a narrow corridor between the railway and the A14. Bridges, locks and watermills provide regular reminders of the river's industrial past but these days the valley is almost totally devoted to leisure. The walk begins at the Barham picnic site, where there is a small visitor centre explaining the history and ecology of the Gipping Valley. The rangers here organise a regular programme of guided walks and events.

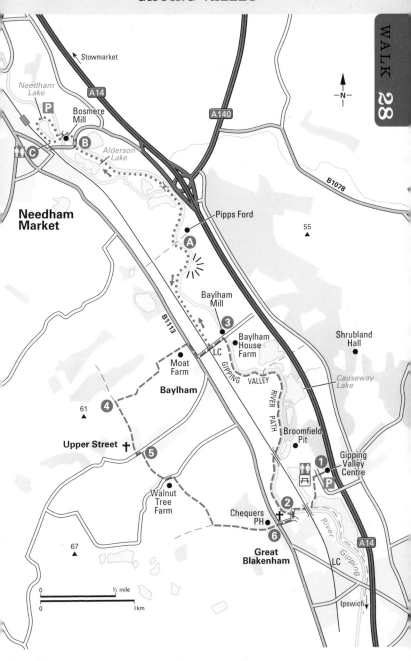

WALK 28 DIRECTIONS

1 Follow the signs from the Gipping Valley Centre to the river. The path crosses a play area, climbs an embankment, crosses a road and descends on the far side. Turn left alongside a fence then bear right between a pair of fishing lakes. Turn right again to walk under a railway bridge and continue along the Gipping Valley River Path.

2 Turn left to cross the bridge at Great Blakenham Lock. Follow the Gipping Valley River Path markers to turn right between the houses and take the narrow passage beside Mill Cottage to return to the river. Stay on this riverside path for 1.5 miles (2.4km). You pass beneath the railway line and cross a quarry access road to come to a wider stretch of river with water-meadows to your left. Pass a lock and keep straight ahead at Causeway Lake. Continue around the edge of a meadow, ignoring a footbridge to the right. Shortly afterwards, cross a stile and bear right, following the course of the river. Walk around another meadow with views of the rare breeds farm, then cross a footbridge and follow a narrow path to Baylham Mill.

WHERE TO EAT AND DRINK

The Chequers at Great Blakenham serves decent pub food and has a children's play area in the garden. Drinks and snacks are also available at Baylham House rare breeds farm and walkers are welcome to use the café without visiting the farm. Alternatively, take a picnic to the picnic site at the start of the walk.

3 Turn left across the bridge. Cross the railway line and turn right at the road. After 200yds (183m), cross the road and walk through the hedge to pass around the back of Moat Farm. Keep straight ahead on a wide track. Turn left then right to climb between fields until you reach a plateau with an isolated oak and sweeping views. Turn left then right on to a field-edge path with hedge to your right.

4 Turn left on a field-edge path to drop into the village of Upper Street. The path swings left through a kissing gate in the hedge and right across a meadow. Go through a gate

WHILE YOU'RE THERE

Baylham House rare breeds farm is located on the site of Combretovium, a strategic Roman fort. Children in particular will enjoy exploring the farm, with its collection of Shetland cattle, Norfolk rams, goats, chickens and kune-kune pigs. The farm is open February to November daily from 11am to 5pm.

and walk down the lane past the church and the old school.

5 At the foot of Church Lane, turn left and immediately right by a sign saying 'No horses please'. The path crosses farmland and briefly enters Devil's Grove before emerging opposite Walnut Tree Farm. Turn left along the lane and right by a pond to pass through a gate and cross a meadow. Go through another gate and keep walking ahead on a cross-field path, then follow the 'circular walk' signs and keep right on a farm track. Turn left to walk into the village of Great Blakenham.

WHAT TO LOOK OUT FOR

Keep an eye out for otters in the River Gipping. According to the rangers, they can easily be confused with mink so you need to know the signs. Adult otters are about twice the length of a domestic cat and have chocolate brown rather than dark brown or black fur. Unlike mink, whose head and body are both visible above water when swimming, the only part of an otter you will see in the water is its head.

6 Cross the B1113 and walk along Mill Lane. The road bends left to return to Point **2**, where you can retrace your steps back to the car park at the start of the walk.

An Extension
To Needham Lake

Continue along the banks of the River Gipping to a popular lake.
See map and information panel for Walk 28

DISTANCE 4.5 miles (7.2km)	MINIMUM TIME 1hr 45min

ASCENT/GRADIENT *Negligible* ▲▲▲ LEVEL OF DIFFICULTY ✦✦✦

PUBLIC TOILETS *Needham Lake*

WALK 29 DIRECTIONS
(Walk 28 option)

This optional extension to Walk 28 takes you further along the Gipping Valley River Path to the small town of Needham Market. Although it's a linear walk, the scenery is so attractive that it is a pleasure to see it again on the way back.

From Point **3**, after crossing the bridge, turn right immediately before the railway line to continue on the Gipping Valley River Path. From here the route is simple as you stay on this path the whole way. At first the path clings to the railway, but it soon drops down beneath the embankment to become a narrow green lane. Follow the path as it bends right to return to the river. The banks are wilder here, heavily overgrown with reeds, thistles and nettles, so long trousers are advisable.

After passing a lock bridge at Pipps Ford, Point **A**, the scenery opens out again with water-meadows to your left. Giant lorries thunder past on the A14 to Felixstowe up ahead. Cross a footbridge, walk past a pylon and continue across a lakeside meadow where cattle and horses graze. Now climb a stile and follow the wide track between the river and Alderson Lake, a popular fishing lake.

Climb to a bridge opposite Bosmere Mill, Point **B**. Turn right to cross the bridge and then left across a meadow, passing the restored Bosmere Lock and a children's playground and picnic area. Walk across the footbridge and turn right to follow the path around Needham Lake. The lake is in a former gravel pit used during the building of the A14. Now it is popular with fishermen, families and model boat enthusiasts and is also a haven for wildlife. Blue tit, chaffinch, grebe and moorhen are all regular visitors. There are frogs, newts, toads, water voles, stoats and grass snakes. A small information office on the south side of the lake, Point **C**, has information on recent sightings.

After making a complete circuit of the lake, return across the footbridge and retrace your steps along the river. As you climb back to the railway embankment, there are good views to your left of Shrubland Hall, a Victorian mansion with earlier gardens designed by the famous landscape gardener 'Capability' Brown.

WALK 30

An Eyeful
of Eye

*An easy walk exploring the surroundings of one
of England's smallest towns.*

DISTANCE 4 miles (6.4km)   MINIMUM TIME 1hr 30min

ASCENT/GRADIENT 98ft (30m) ▲▲▲   LEVEL OF DIFFICULTY ✚✚✚

PATHS *Town streets, farm tracks, woodland paths, 10 stiles*

LANDSCAPE *Farmland, woodland, meadows, town*

SUGGESTED MAP *OS Explorer 230 Diss & Harleston, and town trail available
from dispenser in car park*

START/FINISH *Grid reference: TM 144738*

DOG FRIENDLINESS *Off lead at Town Moor and The Pennings picnic site*

PARKING *Cross Street car park (free), Eye.*

PUBLIC TOILETS *At car park*

WALK 30 DIRECTIONS

Eye was once surrounded by
marshland, hence its name which
derives from the Saxon word for
an island. Although it is officially a
town, Eye feels more like a village
and this short walk will open your
eyes (sorry!) to some of its delights.

Turn right out of the car park
along Cross Street and right again
along Magdalen Street. Turn left
opposite the entrance to Grampian
Country Foods on a footpath that
leads to the playing fields and bear
right around the community centre
to reach a car park. Cross the car
park and go over a footbridge to
enter the Town Moor and Storm
Memorial woodlands, a lovely area
of meadows, ponds, islands, woods
and sculptures created out of the
ruins of the great storm of 1987
that destroyed many trees. Turn left
and keep to the left-hand side of the
woods, passing an 'ash dome' that
is renewed every year and a pond
with a carved wooden lovers' seat
for two people to share. Shortly
afterwards, turn left over a bridge

waymarked 'Eye Country Walks'
to leave the woods and join a field-
edge path.

Turn right at a lane and walk uphill
towards a farm. When you reach an
old barn, cross the stile to your left
and follow the line of the hedge on
your right. When the field narrows,
turn left to cross a footbridge with
a stile on each end and walk across
the meadows. Cross a bridge over
the River Dove and continue across
one more meadow to arrive at a
green lane. Turn left here to walk
between a hedge on your left and
fields on your right. The great

WHERE TO EAT AND DRINK

Beards Tea Room on Church
Street is housed in a delightful
timber-framed cottage and
offers a menu of teas, coffees,
sandwiches, salads, ice creams
and home-made cakes. There
is also a delicatessen next
door where you can stock up
on picnic food. Another good
option is the Queen's Head, a
pink-washed, half-timbered pub
near the start of the walk.

tower of the church at Eye soon comes into view and as the path opens out you will see a group of Norman fish ponds to your left, probably attracting waterfowl such as moorhens, ducks and geese. Pass around a metal barrier and follow the track to the B1077, then cross the road and keep straight ahead on a grassy path.

WHILE YOU'RE THERE

The Thornham Estate at Thornham Parva is the home of Lord and Lady Henniker, who have opened more than 12 miles (19.3km) of waymarked trails on their estate. The walks comprise areas of woodland, parkland and meadows, and there is also a short 0.5 mile (800m) wheelchair trail as well as a walled garden and tea room.

When you reach a lane at the side of a house, take a look at the notice on the wall that threatens a fine of 40 shillings for anyone failing to shut the gate. Turn left and stay on this lane past The Pennings picnic site and nature reserve, in a tranquil setting beside the River Dove. Turn right at the end of the road and in 60yds (55m), turn left along the entrance drive to Abbey Farm, passing the remains of an 11th-century priory, half-hidden in the gardens of the farmhouse.

WHAT TO LOOK OUT FOR

Don't miss the carved figure of the angel Gabriel on a corner post of the Guildhall, that dates from the late 15th century. Another interesting little detail to look out for is the set of inscriptions above the doorways of the almshouses, exhorting their tenants to 'believe right', 'do well' and 'avoid ill for Heaven' and extolling the virtues of 'povertie', 'patience' and 'humilitie'. Charity didn't come without strings attached!

Follow this track past the farm buildings and bear left across a bridge. Continue straight on through a gate to join a field-edge path with hedge to your left. Stay on this track as it bends round to the left, then opens out to reveal good views of Eye across the fields. At the end of the path, turn left through a new housing estate and continue straight ahead beyond the houses on a footpath and cycle path. Keep straight ahead to descend Ash Drive and follow the road right, then left over a footbridge.

Turn right, then left on to the main road. Continue as far as the war memorial and the Victorian red-brick town hall. You could fork right here to return to the car park, but it would be a pity not to explore the town. Turn left along Church Street to follow the course of the old outer bailey of the Norman motte-and-bailey castle that once stood on the castle mound. Pass the school and the timber-framed Guildhall to reach the Church of St Peter and St Paul with its 100ft (30m) tower. Turn right along Castle Street and you will see Castle Hill on your right. In summer you can climb from here to the ruined castle at the top of the mound for views stretching across the border into Norfolk. The keep on the summit is actually a 19th-century folly that was destroyed in a storm in the 1960s. Go back down to Castle Street and turn right to complete your circuit of the town. At the end of this street, turn right into The Cross, where the town's markets once took place, and left before the town hall to return to the start of the walk.

Hoxne and the Death of a King

A walk around the village where the last King of East Anglia met his untimely death.

DISTANCE 3.5 miles (5.7km)   MINIMUM TIME 1hr 30min

ASCENT/GRADIENT 197ft (60m) ▲▲▲   LEVEL OF DIFFICULTY +++

PATHS Country lanes, field and woodland paths, 2 stiles

LANDSCAPE Farmland, woodland and river

SUGGESTED MAP OS Explorer 230 Diss & Harleston

START/FINISH Grid reference: TM 179769

DOG FRIENDLINESS On lead across farmland, off lead in Brakey Wood

PARKING Hoxne village hall

PUBLIC TOILETS None en route

Hoxne, which rhymes with 'oxen', is best known as the place where King Edmund lost his head. Edmund, the last King of East Anglia, born in AD 841, was a Saxon prince who was named by King Offa as his chosen successor. When Offa died on a pilgrimage to the Holy Land, his companions returned to Saxony and brought the young boy home to be crowned King at the age of 14. He reigned peacefully for 15 years, but frequent raids by Danish Vikings unsettled his kingdom and eventually led to all-out war. In AD 870, after a particularly bloody battle, Edmund was captured by the Danes. When he refused to renounce his Christian faith, he was tied to a tree. His body was pelted with arrows and his head was cut off and thrown into the woods.

Betrayed by a Bride

So many legends surround the death of King Edmund that it is difficult to separate fact from fiction. One story tells of the King taking refuge beneath Goldbrook Bridge, which you cross at the start of this walk. A newly married couple spotted his golden spurs reflected in the water and betrayed him to the Danes, thereby ensuring his death. Edmund pronounced a curse on all future brides and to this day people take care to avoid Goldbrook Bridge on their wedding day. A relief sculpture on the outside wall of the nearby village hall shows Edmund crouching beneath the bridge while the bridal party passed overhead.

St Edmund the Martyr

The other colourful story concerns the head itself. Some time after Edmund's death, his followers returned to Hoxne to search for his body. The cries of a howling wolf led them into the forest, where they found the wolf cradling the King's head as if it were her child. A chapel was erected on the spot and became an important shrine, but later his body was moved to Bury St Edmunds. The former King is now known as St Edmund the Martyr and was briefly patron saint of England because of his resistance to the Viking invasion.

Thousand Year Tree
The walk passes close to St Edmund's Monument, which sits in the middle of a field where a huge oak tree once stood. The story goes that the oak collapsed suddenly one night in September 1848, without any apparent cause. Tests showed the tree to be more than 1,000 years old and embedded in its trunk were several iron points which could have been the remains of arrowheads. This evidence could suggest that this could have been the very spot where the good King was murdered.

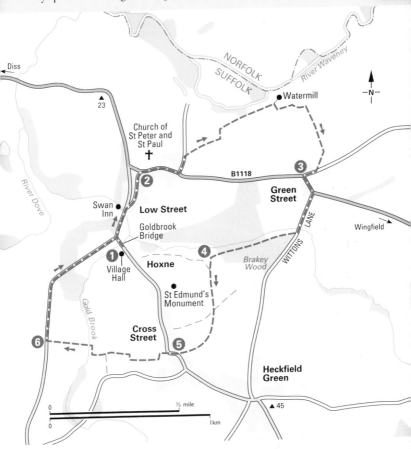

WALK 31 DIRECTIONS

❶ Turn left out of the car park to cross Goldbrook Bridge, noting the inscription on the bridge: 'King Edmund taken prisoner here, AD 870'. Turn right to cross a tributary of the River Dove and pass the Swan Inn on the left. Fork right to climb past the post office alongside the village green and continue to the top of the lane to arrive opposite the Church of St Peter and St Paul.

❷ Turn right along the road and take the second left, Watermill Lane. Bear right along a tarmac and chippings lane with a 'No through road' sign. The lane drops down into a valley beside the water-meadows of the River Waveney which marks the border between Norfolk and Suffolk.

When you reach the entrance drive to the mill, turn right on to another concrete track that swings to the left past some huts to become a green lane bordered by hedges. Turn right on a field-edge path with a house to your left, then right on to a tarmac lane. Turn right at the end of the lane to return to the main road.

WHAT TO LOOK OUT FOR

In Brakey Wood, look for two small groups of sequoia trees which have been planted at either end of the woods. At the moment these are still young, but they are related to the Californian redwood, one of the tallest trees in the world, and should one day grow to a height of over 100ft (30m).

3 Turn left, walk around the bend and turn right on to Wittons Lane, also signposted 'Hoxne Cross Street'. After crossing a stream, turn right through a kissing gate to enter Brakey Wood, a new woodland created to commemorate the millennium. Keep to the right alongside the stream and walk around the edge of the woods before going through a kissing gate to arrive at a sewage works.

4 Keep straight ahead on a footpath along the edge of the field. St Edmund's Monument can

WHERE TO EAT AND DRINK

The Swan at Hoxne is an old timber-framed pub with large riverside gardens that are appreciated both by children and dogs. It serves a good menu of home-cooked food, from simple soups and sandwiches at lunchtime to more elaborate dishes such as baked turbot and mushrooms stuffed with goat's cheese later in the day.

be seen in a field to your right and it is usually possible to reach it on a permissive footpath. Cross a plank footbridge and stay on the public footpath as it bends to the right around a second field and enters a narrow belt of woodland before arriving at Cross Street by the side of a small garage and shop.

5 Maintain your direction, walking straight ahead for another 60yds (55m). When the road bends sharply to the right, continue ahead on a public footpath between the houses which then turns left around a field. The path turns right and left to cross a ditch and drops down steeply beside the next field with a tall hedge on the left-hand side. Cross a stile, turn right and in about 50yds (46m), go left over a footbridge. Pass through a gate and keep walking straight ahead on a sloping cross-field path until you meet a road.

6 Turn right and walk along the road to return to the start of the walk at Goldbrook Bridge.

WHILE YOU'RE THERE

Look into the Church of St Peter and St Paul to see the local history exhibition. There is an interesting display on the Hoxne Hoard, a remarkable find of some 15,000 Roman coins, 29 pieces of gold jewellery and 100 items of silver tableware discovered in a local field in 1992 by a farmer searching for his tools. The hoard now belongs to the British Museum. Also worth a visit is Wingfield College, a 14th-century house near Hoxne with cloisters, walled gardens and contemporary sculpture in the grounds. Check www.wingfieldcollege.com for opening dates – in any event you can also visit the De La Pole Arms, a pub in Wingfield with a reputation for fresh food and local ales.

Stowmarket in the Heart of Suffolk

Rural, urban and industrial landscapes all feature on this walk, together with a fascinating museum.

DISTANCE 6 miles (9.7km)   MINIMUM TIME 2hrs 30min

ASCENT/GRADIENT 213ft (65m) ▲▲▲   LEVEL OF DIFFICULTY ✦✦✦

PATHS Town streets and footpaths, country lanes, field-edge and riverside paths

LANDSCAPE Town, river, farmland and woodland

SUGGESTED MAP OS Explorer 211 Bury St Edmunds & Stowmarket

START/FINISH Grid reference: TM 046585

DOG FRIENDLINESS Dogs should be kept on lead

PARKING Meadow Centre pay-and-display car park, Stowmarket (follow signs to Museum of East Anglian Life)

PUBLIC TOILETS At Meadow Centre

Stowmarket, right in the centre of Suffolk, is a typically attractive and prosperous market town that has developed to encompass a healthy mix of farming, industry and trade. This makes it a fitting home for the Museum of East Anglian Life, a 70-acre (28ha) open-air museum in the grounds of the former Abbot's Hall Estate.

Museum of East Anglian Life

The museum tells the story of the people of East Anglia through displays on agriculture, work and domestic life. Among the exhibits are a recreated Victorian kitchen, an old schoolroom and a collection of gypsy caravans. There are regular demonstrations of blacksmithing and charcoal-making, as well as harvesting in summer. There are also Suffolk Punch horses, local breeds of sheep and pigs, meadows, wildflower gardens and a walk beside the River Rat (which sounds like a character out of Toad of Toad Hall, but is in fact the local name for the Rattlesden).

Rescued Buildings

However, what makes the museum really interesting is its collection of old buildings. Apart from the 14th-century tithe barn near the entrance, which houses a display of farming tools, all of the buildings have been moved here from elsewhere. The oldest is the 14th-century aisled hall of Edgar's Farmhouse, rescued from the neighbouring village of Combs when it was threatened by a housing development in 1971. The roof beams of this half-timbered farmhouse are still coated in soot from the fire that once burned in the open hearth.

Other buildings include a wind pump that was used to drain water from the Minsmere marshes, an 18th-century blacksmith's forge, a watermill, a chapel and a 19th-century factory building containing exhibits relating to East Anglia's industrial heritage.

Exhibits in the recently constructed William Bone Building tell the story of Ransomes, the company founded by Robert Ransome, which began in

STOWMARKET

1789 as a two-man foundry in Ipswich and grew to become one of the biggest producers of agricultural machinery in the world. Ransomes lawnmowers, which included the first petrol mower and the first electric mower ever to be produced, were used on tennis courts and golf courses, at Kew Gardens and Regent's Park, and exported to countries from Russia to Argentina. In 1998, the company was sold to the American corporation Textron but it continues to operate a factory in Suffolk.

The industries of East Anglia were traditionally rural crafts, such as brewing, basket making, rope making and tanning. This last craft was particularly important in Combs. This walk takes you across farmland between Stowmarket and Combs, then ends with a riverside stretch by one of the biggest paint factories in the world. It may not be particularly pretty, but ICI is as much a part of Stowmarket's history as the river, the railway, the maltings and the farm.

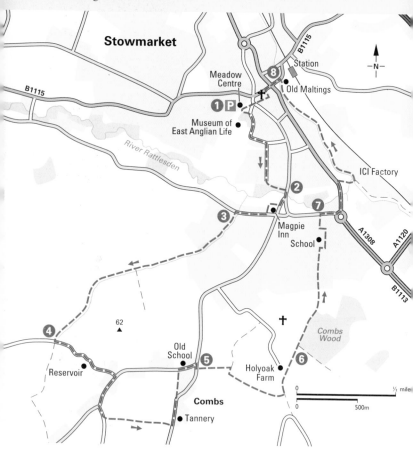

WALK 32 DIRECTIONS

❶ From the car park, take the path that runs past the museum and the gates of Abbot's Hall. When the path divides, fork right alongside a high

brick wall, then turn right along a lane. At the end of the lane, turn left and look for a narrow path between the houses on the right, just before No. 19. Stay on this path as it drops down to the river, then turn left

WHILE YOU'RE THERE

The Museum of East Anglian Life is open daily from April to October, with limited opening hours in winter. Allow at least two hours. You should also allow time for a walk around Combs Wood, a Suffolk Wildlife Trust nature reserve with wild flowers and shady woodland rides. Dogs are not allowed in the reserve.

along a wide lane between houses and the River Rattlesden.

2 Reaching a road, turn right across the bridge and fork right when the road divides. Just before the Magpie Inn, turn right through the shopping precinct to reach Combs Lane. Cross the road and walk along the pavement until you cross a small stream just beyond Edgecomb Road.

3 Turn left at the stream by a telegraph pole with a 'Charcoal and Churches' circular walk sign. The path follows the stream then heads through a wood and into open countryside. Cross a footbridge and turn right along a field-edge path.

4 At a metal barrier, turn left along a tarmac lane, past a mobile phone tower and reservoir. Turn right at the T-junction, then fork left along Mill Lane. After 70yds (64m), turn left on a path that runs between parkland and fields. Turn left at the road to pass an old tannery, then head left on a tarmac path at Webb's Close to climb to the centre of Combs. Turn right at the road and walk past the old village school.

5 At the junction, turn right and immediately left, dropping down between the fields. Cross a footbridge and follow a field-edge path to the right. Go through a gate and bear diagonally across the field to reach a junction where you turn

left, passing a thatched farmhouse on your way to Combs Wood.

6 Stay on this path as it runs alongside the wood and into a housing estate. Continue straight ahead on the paved path, crossing Lavenham Way and diverting around a school, turning left at the bottom, then right.

WHERE TO EAT AND DRINK

The Museum of East Anglian Life has a bistro and tea room open to non-museum patrons, offering a range of sandwiches, jacket potatoes, salads and hot dishes. The Magpie Inn is on the walk itself, while other pubs and cafés can be found in the town centre.

7 Turn right on Needham Road, then left along Gipping Way. Just before the paint factory, turn right, cross a bridge and go left on the signed Gipping Valley River Path. Follow this path to the old maltings.

8 Climb the steps to the bridge and turn left along Station Road. Keep straight ahead at the crossroads, then go left through the churchyard. Narrow Buttermarket leads to the Market Place. Cross the square and walk through the Meadow Centre to the car park.

WHAT TO LOOK OUT FOR

There are several interesting features in Stowmarket. Notice the town clock in the Market Place, erected above the post office (now a bookmaker) by public subscription in the late 19th century, when the clock in the church tower was proving unreliable. The church itself has a modern copper spire, built in 1993 as a replica of an earlier version. Stowmarket Station was built in 1849 and is considered one of the finest Victorian stations in England. It's still in use, on the London-to-Norwich line.

The Mills of Pakenham

*Visit a working watermill on an easy walk
around gentle farmland.*

> **DISTANCE** *4.5 miles (7.2km)* **MINIMUM TIME** *1hr 45min*
> **ASCENT/GRADIENT** *164ft (50m)* ▲▲▲ **LEVEL OF DIFFICULTY** ✚✚✚
> **PATHS** *Bridleways, field-edge paths and quiet country lanes*
> **LANDSCAPE** *Rolling farmland around Ixworth village*
> **SUGGESTED MAP** *OS Explorers 211 Bury St Edmunds & Stowmarket;
> 229 Thetford Forest in the Brecks*
> **START/FINISH** *Grid reference: TL 932703 (on Explorer 229)*
> **DOG FRIENDLINESS** *Farmland – dogs on lead*
> **PARKING** *Ixworth village hall free car park*
> **PUBLIC TOILETS** *At car park, beside library*

At one time, almost every village in Suffolk had a windmill, grinding corn to produce flour for the local bakery. Their turning sails were a familiar feature of the rural landscape but one that is rarely seen these days. Of 500 mills which existed at the start of the 19th century, fewer than 40 remain and only half of these retain their machinery. Others have been converted into modern houses and the majority have disappeared through neglect.

In recent years, however, there has been a movement to restore and maintain the last remaining mills. Pakenham, near Bury St Edmunds, is now the only parish in England with a working windmill and watermill. The latter, owned by the Suffolk Preservation Trust, can be visited from Easter to September on Wednesdays and at weekends, when the waterwheel turns and the machinery cranks into action to produce genuine stoneground flour.

A mill has stood on this site since the time of the Domesday Book in 1086 and it is possible that the Romans also milled grain here as they are known to have built a fort in the area. The enthusiastic curators will show you around the mill, explaining how water is released from the mill pond to turn the 16ft (5m) wheel, and pointing out obscure industrial features like the 'wallower', the 'damsel' and the Blackstone oil engine, dating from 1904.

From the garden beside the mill pond there are views across the fen to Pakenham Windmill, a five-storey brick tower mill built in 1816 and recently restored to working order. Pakenham is on the Miller's Trail, a signposted circuit of Suffolk villages that takes in half a dozen mills. Among the mills that can be visited in summer are the watermill at Euston, the post mill at Stanton and the tower mill at Thelnetham, which also produces its own organic flour. You can pick up a map of the Miller's Trail at Pakenham Watermill.

Although the two mills are officially in Pakenham, they are closer to Ixworth, where this walk begins. Ixworth is on the site of a major Iceni settlement and also a Roman fort, strategically situated at the junction of the Bury St Edmunds to Norwich and Ipswich to Thetford roads. A modern bypass keeps most traffic away and the result is a quiet village of timber-framed houses along the High Street, which retains a selection of shops and pubs.

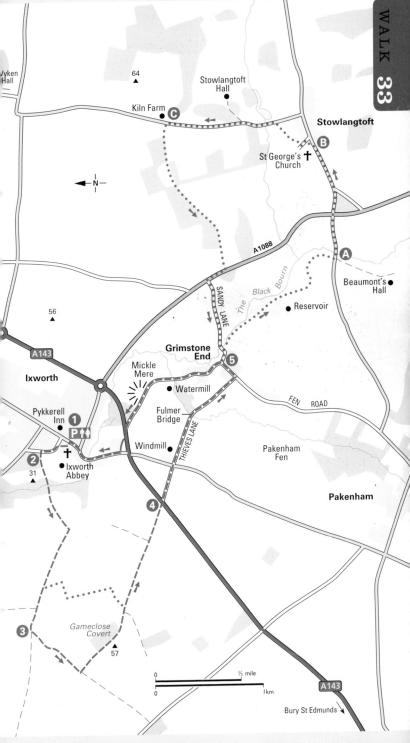

Vyken
Hall

64 ▲

Stowlangtoft
Hall

Kiln Farm ● **C**

Stowlangtoft

St George's **B**
Church ✝

← N →

A1088

A

Beaumont's
Hall

56 ▲

The Black Bourn

● Reservoir

SANDY LANE

**Grimstone
End**

5

A143

Ixworth

Mickle
Mere

● Watermill

FEN ROAD

Pykkerell
Inn ● **1**
P ♦♦

✝
● Ixworth
Abbey

2

31 ▲

Fulmer
Bridge

● Windmill

THIEVES LANE

Pakenham
Fen

Pakenham

4

3

Gameclose
Covert

57 ▲

0 ½ mile
0 1km

A143

Bury St Edmunds ↘

WALK 33 DIRECTIONS

1 Leaving the village hall car park, cross the High Street and take the path that leads through the churchyard around the right of the parish church. Turn left on to Commister Lane and follow this road as it bends round to the right.

2 Turn left on to a bridle path opposite Abbey Close. Looking left from this broad, tree-lined path, there are good views of Ixworth Abbey, a Georgian manor built around the ruins of a 12th-century Augustinian priory and incorporating the crypt of the original monastery into its design. Stay on this path as it crosses the Black Bourn and makes its way towards a small wood, where it swings right. A footpath on your left after 600yds (549m) gives you the option of a short cut across the fields. For the full walk, keep straight on towards Point **3**.

3 Turn left at the end of a hedgerow and follow this field-edge path until you see a metal gate ahead. Turn left here on to a farm track that passes around a wood. Soon after the wood, the short cut rejoins the main walk from your left and you get your first glimpse of Pakenham Windmill up ahead. Keep straight ahead on this track to reach the main road, the A143.

4 Cross the road carefully and go straight ahead to another crossroads, where you keep straight ahead to reach the windmill. Stay on this narrow road, known as Thieves Lane, as it drops down to Fulmer Bridge, a bucolic spot of meadows and streams. Continue towards a T-junction, then turn left along Fen Road, passing a group of council houses and bungalows before reaching a junction at the foot of the hill.

5 Stay on Fen Road as it bends round to the left into the small hamlet of Grimstone End where you soon reach Pakenham Watermill. Just beyond the watermill, there are views of Mickle Mere, a popular birding spot, to your right. Stay on this road to return to the A143, where you turn left along a pavement path before crossing the main road at a white post to reach a quiet lane on the far side. Turn left here and when you get to the end of the lane, turn right and follow the road into Ixworth to return to the car park.

Stately Stowlangtoft

An optional loop through typical Suffolk countryside to Stowlangtoft.
See map and information panel for Walk 33

DISTANCE *4 miles (6.4km)*	MINIMUM TIME *1hr 30min*
ASCENT/GRADIENT *115ft (35m)* ▲▲▲	LEVEL OF DIFFICULTY +++

WALK 34 DIRECTIONS (Walk 33 option)

At Point **5** on the main walk, where Fen Road swings round to the left, turn right instead. Almost immediately the road bends left over a bridge, but you keep ahead on a field-edge path, with the Black Bourn just visible behind a hedge to your left. Stay on this path as it crosses to the other side of the hedge and runs across the top of a meadow with the Black Bourn hidden beside a covert at the far side of the field.

Pass a stile as you leave the meadow, and you soon reach open countryside, with arable fields ahead and a reservoir behind an embankment on your right. The path runs straight across the field, with a single large tree ahead, then enters a small meadow with stiles at either end before turning left around a field. Soon you reach a minor road opposite the entrance to Beaumont's Hall farm, Point **A**.

Turn left, cross a bridge and keep straight ahead at the junction with the A1088. Stay on this road as it climbs gently into Stowlangtoft. When you reach St George's Church, Point **B**, leave the road to walk through the churchyard. This brings you out on to Church View. Turn left and look for a grassy path between the houses to the right. At the end of this path, cross a stile and bear right across a meadow, passing through a kissing gate to emerge beside a pumping station. Turn left here and you will soon see Stowlangtoft Hall, a Victorian mansion now used as a nursing home, through the trees to your right. Pass the entrance to the hall and stay on this lane as it ascends the hill.

> ### WHILE YOU'RE THERE
> The notice-board outside St George's Church gives details of the keyholders, and it is worth looking inside the church to admire the magnificent carved benches in the nave.

At Kiln Farm, Point **C**, turn left on to a footpath that passes a barn, enters a plantation and crosses a meadow before reaching a wide open stretch with views across the fields to Stowlangtoft church. When you reach the A1088, turn right and walk along this road for about 200yds (183m), taking care as there is no pavement and only a narrow grass verge. Cross the road and turn left on to Sandy Lane. Stay on this lane as it bends round to the left, crossing Baileypool Bridge to return to Point **5**.

Knettishall Heath Country Park

Explore the diverse landscapes and wildlife of Suffolk's largest country park.

DISTANCE	4 miles (6.4km)
MINIMUM TIME	1hr 30min
ASCENT/GRADIENT	164ft (50m) ▲▲▲
LEVEL OF DIFFICULTY	✦✦✦
PATHS	Well-marked country park trails
LANDSCAPE	Heathland, grassland, woodland, meadows, river
SUGGESTED MAP	Map of country park available from information office
START/FINISH	Grid reference: TL 955807
DOG FRIENDLINESS	Well-controlled dogs welcome in country park
PARKING	Knettishall Heath Country Park main car park
PUBLIC TOILETS	At car park

WALK 35 DIRECTIONS

This is the only walk in this book that is situated entirely within a country park. Although this might seem an unadventurous choice, the landscapes of heathland, grassland, woodland and river are considerably more varied than you are likely to encounter on most walks in rural Suffolk. Unlike farmland, which is expected to produce a profit, a country park can be managed for both conservation and recreation with the result that a wide variety of habitats can be protected. On this walk you will see semi-wild Exmoor ponies grazing on the heath, you may spot lizards, butterflies and muntjac deer, or see wild flowers such as red campion, rock rose, honeysuckle and wild thyme in summer.

Knettishall Heath Country Park is found in the far north of Suffolk, in the area known as the Brecks. Whatever it may look like, this is a landscape created by human activity over many thousands of years. Bronze Age farmers kept sheep on the grasslands and cultivated the fields. More recently, rabbit warrens were built to breed rabbits for their meat and fur, helping at the same time to keep the grass down. It's only since World War Two and the arrival of myxomatosis that the heath has been left to its own devices. Without careful management it would revert to woodland and scrub within about 50 years.

This walk follows the waymarked trails that have been set out in the country park, and which are clearly marked on a map available

WHAT TO LOOK OUT FOR

The Exmoor ponies that graze on Knettishall Heath are the surviving descendants of a breed of wild horse that arrived in Britain more than 130,000 years ago. These hardy creatures have survived almost untamed and have adapted over the centuries to develop thick coats and large teeth that help them to cope with their conditions. They are kept on the heathland because regular grazing helps to prevent the invasion of bracken and scrub.

from the information office in the car park. The Riverside Trail is waymarked in blue with the symbol of flowing water. The red and green Heathland Trails are waymarked with the sign of a rabbit, while the yellow Woodland Trail takes an oak tree as its symbol. The walk covers sections of all three trails, but you could easily design your own walk instead.

Start by following the Riverside Trail, clearly signposted from the information office and toilet block. The trail takes you down to the banks of the Little Ouse River that divides Suffolk from Norfolk. After about 0.5 mile (800m), the trail turns away from the river between areas of woodland and meadow. When the trail turns sharp left after crossing a footbridge, leave the Riverside Trail and go right instead, to head towards the woods.

Now you are on the green Heathland Trail, though frustratingly the waymarking posts are only marked on one side and you are walking in the opposite direction. Turn left at a junction of paths and continue down to the road along the western boundary of the park. This is the end of the Peddars Way, a National Trail that follows a Roman road to the North Norfolk coast, and the start of the Icknield Way, possibly the oldest route in Britain. Cross the car park and continue along

the path that soon arrives at open heathland covered with purple heather in summer. Turn left along the edge of a line of fir trees and bear left, still on the green trail, around the edge of the heath. Turn right at a junction of paths to reach the remains of an 18th-century rabbit warren. Keep straight ahead at a crossroads and continue to the end of this path, then bear left towards Hut Hill, a Bronze Age burial mound that dates back to 2000 BC and is easily identified by the lone Scots pine at its summit. Keeping the burial mound to your right, walk down the hill, then turn sharp right at a junction to join the yellow Woodland Trail. For a short cut you could keep straight ahead to return to the car park at this point.

You now stay on the Woodland Trail for the remainder of your walk as it weaves its way through the woods past silver birch, oak and Scots pine. The path briefly joins a horse route and passes a barrier to reach a road. Cross the road and continue on a path to your left. Towards the end of the trail you pass an area of grazed heathland where Exmoor ponies and Hebridean sheep are kept. Cross the road again, turn right through a woody glade and continue to the car park, where there is a small playground and a weir where children splash about in the river.

Oil on Canvas at
Sudbury Common Lands

*Stroll among the peaceful grazing cattle
and visit the home of a famous 18th-century artist.*

DISTANCE 5 miles (8km)   MINIMUM TIME 2hrs

ASCENT/GRADIENT Negligible ▲▲▲   LEVEL OF DIFFICULTY +++

PATHS Old railway track, meadows and town streets

LANDSCAPE Sudbury and water-meadows of River Stour

SUGGESTED MAP OS Explorer 196 Sudbury, Hadleigh & Dedham Vale

START/FINISH Grid reference: TL 875409

DOG FRIENDLINESS Off lead on Valley Walk, on lead on Sudbury Common

PARKING Kingfisher Leisure Centre (free)

PUBLIC TOILETS Off Market Hill

The market town of Sudbury has a unique feature on its doorstep. The Sudbury Common Lands make up some 115 acres (46.5ha) of picturesque water-meadows on the flood plain of the River Stour. Cattle and horses graze here, as they have for more than a 1,000 years, and the area is crossed by footpaths, making it perfect for a peaceful walk. Anywhere else, the land would have been swallowed up by housing or intensive farming, but here in Sudbury it is protected by ancient right, a large area of grassland close to the centre of town.

The water-meadows of Sudbury were first mentioned in the Domesday Book of 1086. Their current status dates from around 1260, when the Freemen of Sudbury acquired grazing rights from Richard de Clare, the owner of Clare Castle. The right to graze livestock on the commons still belongs exclusively to the freemen, passed on over the generations from father to son.

Thomas Gainsborough

The artist Thomas Gainsborough (1727–88) was born in Sudbury and as a boy he used to wander these meadows looking for inspiration. Both his father, a cloth dealer, and his uncle, who ran the local grammar school, were Freemen of the Commons. It is said that young Thomas would often play truant from school in order to sketch in the countryside. Although he later became better known as a portrait painter, Gainsborough loved to paint landscapes and his society portraits were simply a way of earning enough money to survive.

Gainsborough's House, in a Georgian-fronted brick building close to Market Hill, has been restored and opened as a museum. It contains the most complete collection of his work on display anywhere in the world, including his first known portraits of a boy and a girl, a miniature of his wife, and some 20 portraits of rich clergymen, politicians and landowners. A small cabinet holds Gainsborough's personal items, such as his pocket watch, snuff box, pipe stopper and paint scraper. The walled garden, where exhibitions of sculpture are held in summer, contains a 400-year-old mulberry tree.

SUDBURY

The walk begins with a section of the Valley Walk, along the disused railway line to Bury St Edmunds and Cambridge. This is not a public right of way but it is maintained by Suffolk County Council and walkers are encouraged. Bramble, hawthorn and oak grow beside the embankments, which also attract a wide variety of birds, insects and wild flowers. Note the contrast between the featureless arable fields to the left and the richness of the water-meadows to the right. It certainly makes you appreciate how fortunate the people of Sudbury are to have managed to preserve such a precious landscape.

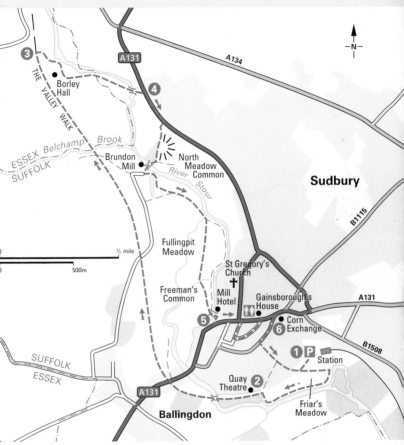

WALK 36 DIRECTIONS

1 Leave the car park at the Kingfisher Leisure Centre through a gate at the start of the Valley Walk, then turn left to walk around Friar's Meadow. Cross the meadow and turn right to follow the bank of the Stour, then turn right alongside a tributary and climb the steps to rejoin the Valley Walk.

2 Turn left and cross a footbridge, noting the Quay Theatre, housed in the town's old maltings, to your right. You now stay on the Valley Walk for a further 2 miles (3.2km). At first the path is enclosed between tall embankments but, after passing a Stour Valley Path sign and crossing Belchamp Brook, it opens out to reveal views of arable farmland and meadows.

❸ Just before reaching a road junction, climb the steps of the embankment on the right, cross a paddock and turn right along the driveway to Borley Hall. Look for a narrow footpath between the high garden wall of the hall and Borley Mill, the first of three former watermills on this route. Go through a gate to cross a small meadow to a further gate, then turn left beside a stream. Cross a footbridge and walk across a meadow to reach a road at the end of an enclosed path.

❹ Turn right along the pavement for 250yds (229m). Just beyond Chaucer Road on your left, turn right on to a tarmac lane with views of North Meadow Common to your left. Cross the bridge to pass Brundon Mill and turn left alongside a row of pink cottages. Soon you are on the Sudbury Common Lands among the horses and cattle. Walk across the meadow,

passing a World War Two pill box, then cross a footbridge and bear half right across Fullingpit Meadow. A metal bridge leads into Freemen's Common, where you bear half right towards the old white-painted mill, now converted into the Mill Hotel.

❺ Pass through the gate to walk beside the hotel, then turn right and left along Stour Street, passing several half-timbered buildings including the 15th-century Salters Hall. Turn right along School Street past the old grammar school, then left along Christopher Lane to emerge on Gainsborough Street opposite Gainsborough's House. Turn right to reach Market Hill, where a statue of Thomas Gainsborough stands in front of St Peter's Church.

❻ Turn right past the 19th-century Corn Exchange, now a library, along Friars Street. After passing half-timbered Buzzards Hall, once owned by Gainsborough's uncle, look for a passage on the left that leads back down to the start of the Valley Walk.

The Tudors of Long Melford

A walk through farmland and woods,
by a Tudor mansion and a fine church.

DISTANCE 6 miles (9.7km)	MINIMUM TIME 2hrs 45min

ASCENT/GRADIENT 213ft (65m) ▲▲▲ LEVEL OF DIFFICULTY ✦✦✦

PATHS Farm tracks, field and woodland paths, 7 stiles

LANDSCAPE Farmland, woodland and views of Holy Trinity Church

SUGGESTED MAP OS Explorer 196 Sudbury, Hadleigh & Dedham Vale

START/FINISH Grid reference: TL 864465

DOG FRIENDLINESS On lead across farmland

PARKING Church Walk, Long Melford

PUBLIC TOILETS By village green, Gatehouse of Kentwell Hall (when open)

During the 15th century while much of England was in economic decline, the wool towns of South Suffolk prospered on the lucrative trade in wool, cloth and silk. Among the legacies of this period are the so-called 'wool churches', financed by rich merchants and built in the Perpendicular style. Some of these churches are cathedral-like in their stature. There are fine wool churches at Lavenham, Sudbury, Cavendish and Clare, but perhaps the greatest of all is Holy Trinity Church, Long Melford.

Wool Church

The church stands alone at the top of the green, utterly dominating its surroundings. This is the only parish church in England to have its own separate Lady Chapel, a feature normally reserved for cathedrals and abbeys (look at the multiplication tables painted on to the wall, that show that the Lady Chapel was also once the village school). The north aisle of the church contains some of the finest 15th-century stained glass in England. Look for the 'rabbit window' above the north door, featuring three rabbits sharing three ears, thought to be a reference to the Holy Trinity.

Sir William Cordell

Long Melford means 'long mill ford' and the village boasts the longest main street in England, running south from the green for almost 2 miles (3.2km). Two names crop up repeatedly in the history of the village. Sir William Cordell was a Speaker of the House of Commons who was granted the manor of Melford after the Dissolution of the Monasteries – it had previously been a hunting estate for the monks of Bury St Edmunds Abbey. He built Melford Hall, where he entertained Queen Elizabeth I in 1578, and he was also responsible for the founding of Trinity Hospital for '12 poor men' in 1573. His richly carved tomb can be seen in the chancel of the church.

The other great Melford family were the Cloptons of Kentwell Hall. It was John Clopton, a clothier, who helped to fund the church and it is full of monuments to his family, including a recumbent statue of Sir William Clopton, 'whose door was ever open to the poor.' The Cloptons had their

WALK 37

own entrance to the church and their own chantry chapel, even their own separate font for holy water, cleverly set into Sir William Clopton's tomb.

Kentwell Hall has now been revived as a living history museum. Don't be surprised to see monks, merchants and maidens in Elizabethan costume as you glance over the wall during one of the regular recreations of Tudor life.

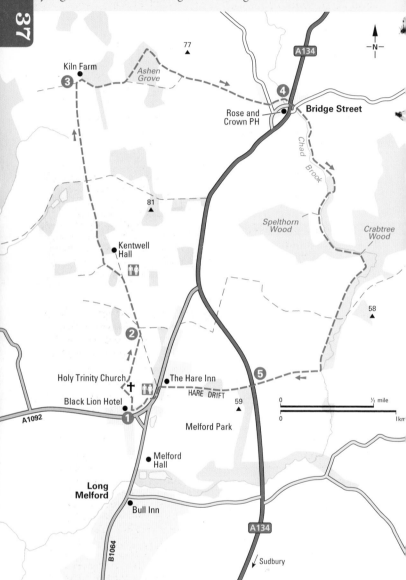

WALK 37 DIRECTIONS

1 Starting from the Black Lion Hotel, walk up the west side of the green towards the church,

passing the almshouses of Trinity Hospital on the way. Bear left around the church and walk through the rectory garden. Cross a stile, then turn right in a

LONG MELFORD

few paces and cross a paddock, heading for the stile in the corner. Cross another stile to reach a meadow and continue straight ahead until you reach the long drive to Kentwell Hall.

2 Turn left and walk beside the avenue of lime trees towards Kentwell Hall. When you reach the main gate, turn left to walk through the grounds with good views of the hall. Follow the waymarks to turn right beside a hedge and continue straight ahead on a wide track that crosses farmland with sweeping views to both sides. Ignore tracks leading off to right and left and continue towards Kiln Farm.

3 Just before the derelict farm buildings, turn right on to a track running between the fields and the woods. At the second wood, Ashen Grove, turn left on to a shady woodland path that crosses two grassy tracks and swings right through the trees to emerge on to a field-edge path. Continue straight ahead on a cross-field path, that cuts through a hedge and makes its way across the fields towards Bridge Street. Cross a lane and walk past a recreation ground, then go over a pair of stiles to reach the A134 by the Rose and Crown pub.

4 Cross the main road carefully and take the left fork opposite. Almost immediately, turn right on to a path alongside Chad Brook. Stay on this path for about 1.75 miles (2.8km) as it crosses a footbridge to the west side of the brook, then clings to the stream between farmland to the right and woodland to the left. Ignore the first path off to the right. At the end of the woods, the path suddenly swings right to climb around the edge of a field and return to the A134.

WHAT TO LOOK OUT FOR

On the green at Long Melford is a red-brick Elizabethan conduit, built around 1550 to supply water to Melford Hall and to the village. The grassy area around the conduit is left unmown in order to attract wild flowers such as orchids and cuckooflowers.

5 Cross the road again and keep straight ahead along Hare Drift, now a concrete track. You reach Long Melford between a garden centre and a pub, directly opposite the entrance to Kentwell Hall. Cross the road, turn left and walk back down towards the green.

WHILE YOU'RE THERE

It would be a shame to visit Long Melford without looking in at Kentwell Hall, especially if you are there during one of the recreations of Tudor life that take place at bank holiday weekends and over several weeks in June and July. The village's other Tudor mansion, Melford Hall, is a National Trust property with landscaped gardens, a panelled banqueting hall and a room devoted to the children's author Beatrix Potter, who was a frequent visitor to the hall.

Lavenham Wool Town

*Explore the rolling countryside around
one of Suffolk's prettiest towns.*

DISTANCE 5.5 miles (8.8km)   MINIMUM TIME 2hrs 30min

ASCENT/GRADIENT 197ft (60m) ▲▲▲   LEVEL OF DIFFICULTY ✦✦✦

PATHS Field-edge paths and tracks, some stretches of road

LANDSCAPE Rolling farmland and attractive town

SUGGESTED MAP OS Explorers 196 Sudbury, Hadleigh & Dedham Vale;
211 Bury St Edmunds & Stowmarket

START/FINISH Grid reference: TL 914489 (on Explorer 196)

DOG FRIENDLINESS Farmland – keep dogs under control

PARKING Church Street car park (free), Lavenham

PUBLIC TOILETS At car park

Lavenham is possibly the best-preserved medieval town in England. During the 15th and 16th centuries it grew rich on the wool trade, exporting cloth to Europe, Africa and Asia. At one time its people paid more in taxes than those of Lincoln and York. Merchants and clothiers built the half-timbered houses that still attract visitors today. At times, when tourist coaches clog the High Street, Lavenham is just too pretty for its own good.

Lavenham is an open-air museum of medieval architecture. When the wool trade declined, nothing took its place, with the result that the town centre retains its medieval street plan, a network of lanes fanning out from the market square with its 16th-century cross. Entire streets, such as Water Street, are lined with crooked, half-timbered houses, delicately colour-washed in ochre, mustard and Suffolk pink. Look out, too, for the pargeting such as the Tudor rose and fleur-de-lis on the façade of the Swan Inn.

Famous Inhabitants

The artist John Constable went to school here, at the Old Grammar School in Barn Street. One of his friends was Jane Taylor, who wrote the nursery rhyme 'Twinkle, Twinkle Little Star' (1806) at nearby Shilling Grange. But the biggest name in Lavenham's history has been that of the de Vere family. Aubrey de Vere was granted the manor by his brother-in-law William the Conqueror. Four centuries later, John de Vere, 13th Earl of Oxford, led Henry VII's victorious army at the Battle of Bosworth in 1485. This was the final battle of the Wars of the Roses and it was in thanks for his safe return that local merchants built the parish church of St Peter and St Paul. One of the largest parish churches in England, its 141ft (43m) flint tower dominates the skyline. With its rich Gothic tracery, coffered roof, graceful arches, columns and aisles, it is also one of the finest examples of the Perpendicular style.

This walk combines a visit to Lavenham with a gentle country stroll. To give yourself time to explore the town, follow the main walk out into the

LAVENHAM

fields on either side of a broad river valley before ending up at the market square where you can visit the Guildhall and wander the medieval lanes. For a longer walk, extend the route by taking Walk 39 to reach the two delightful villages of Kettlebaston and Preston St Mary to the north-east – and still be back at Lavenham in time for tea.

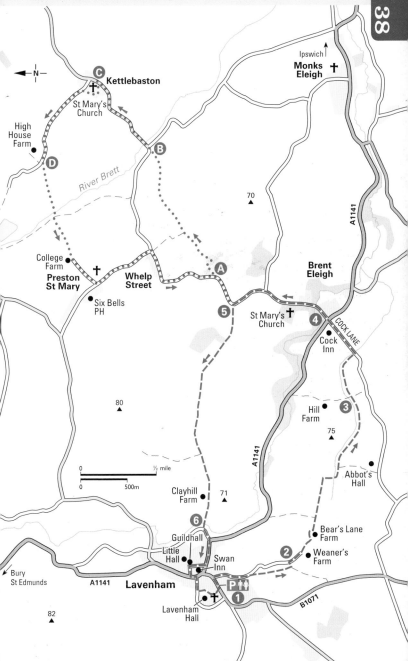

Kettlebaston

St Mary's Church

High House Farm

River Brett

College Farm

Preston St Mary

Six Bells PH

Whelp Street

Monks Eleigh

Ipswich

70 ▲

Brent Eleigh

St Mary's Church

COCK LANE

Cock Inn

A1141

Hill Farm

75 ▲

Abbot's Hall

80 ▲

Clayhill Farm

71 ▲

Bear's Lane Farm

Weaner's Farm

Guildhall

Little Hall

Swan Inn

Bury St Edmunds

A1141

Lavenham

Lavenham Hall

82 ▲

B1071

0   ½ mile

0   500m

Overleaf: Detail of timber work on the 14th-century Little Hall at Lavenham (Walk 38)

109

WALK 38

WALK 38 DIRECTIONS

1 Turn right out of the car park and go down the hill into town. At the first junction, turn right along Bear's Lane. Continue on this road for 0.25 mile (400m) until the last house, then take the footpath to the right across fields. After another field boundary in 0.25 mile (400m), turn left in the next field and follow a ditch to rejoin the road.

2 Turn right and walk past Weaner's Farm. Turn left at a footpath sign just before a converted barn. Stay on this path as it swings around Bear's Lane Farm, then turn left on to a track beside a hedge. Walk along this track as it bears right to the valley bottom. When the track bends right towards Abbot's Hall, keep straight ahead and fork to the right on a grassy path beside a stream.

3 Emerging from a poplar grove, you arrive at a concrete drive where you must turn right and immediately left. The path swings round to the right to reach a road, Cock Lane. Turn left and stay on this road as it climbs and then descends to a crossroads.

4 Cross the A1141 into Brent Eleigh. When the road bends, with the village hall and half-timbered Corner Farm to your right, keep straight ahead to climb to St Mary's Church. Look into the church to see the late 13th-century wall paintings and 17th-century box pews. Continue up the same road.

5 When the road swings sharply to the right, look for a path on the left. Stay on this path for about 1.25 miles (2km) as it winds between tall hedges with occasional glimpses of open countryside. Emerging into the daylight, there is a wonderful view of the church tower at Lavenham standing proudly above the town. Walk past Clayhill Farm and descend into the valley, crossing a white-painted bridge.

6 Turn left at the junction and walk into Lavenham along Water Street, with its fine timber-framed houses. Just after Lavenham Priory on your left, turn right up Lady Street, passing the tourist office on the way to the market place. Turn left down narrow Market Lane to arrive at the High Street opposite the picturesque Crooked House. Turn briefly left and then right along Hall Road. Before the road bends, look for a footpath on the left, then walk through a meadow to reach Lavenham church. The car park is across the road.

Kettlebaston and Preston St Mary

An additional loop in the hills above Lavenham, taking in two small villages.
See map and information panel for Walk 38

DISTANCE *4.5 miles (7.2km)* MINIMUM TIME *2hrs*

ASCENT/GRADIENT *312ft (95m)* ▲▲▲ LEVEL OF DIFFICULTY ✦✦✦

PATHS *I stile*

WALK 39 DIRECTIONS (Walk 38 option)

To extend Walk 38, keep to the road at Point **5** as it swings round to the right. At the next bend, Point **A**, turn right along a wide grassy track. There are fields on both sides at first, then a hedge, and eventually the track becomes a tarmac lane. After 1 mile (1.6km) you reach a road junction, Point **B**. Keep straight ahead, cross a bridge and climb the hill into Kettlebaston to arrive at St Mary's Church, which is Point **C**.

Opposite the church, the village sign features two crossed sceptres, one gold, the other ivory, topped by a pair of doves. This is a reference to William de la Pole, Marquis of Suffolk, who was granted the manor of Kettlebaston by Henry VI on condition that he bear a sceptre (gold for a king, ivory for a queen) at all royal coronations. Turn left to enter the church through an archway of yews. At the back of the church are some casts of the 14th-century Kettlebaston Alabasters, depicting the Coronation of Mary, the Annunciation, Ascension and Holy Trinity. The originals were discovered in the chancel wall in 1864 and are now in the British Museum in London. Among the other treasures is the 20th-century rood screen with portraits of English saints.

Walk through the churchyard and turn right behind the church, cross a meadow and climb over a stile to reach a lane. Turn left and walk along this lane for 0.5 mile (800m) between stud and cattle farms. Just before the entrance to High House Farm, Point **D**, turn left on to a field-edge path running beside a ditch. At the foot of the field, cross a wooden bridge to join a path on the other side of the stream. Follow this path round to the right between paddocks then go through a gate and walk uphill on a concrete lane to College Farm.

After passing the farm, the lane becomes a road leading into Preston St Mary. Look for a gate in the hedge on your left to enter St Mary's churchyard. Leave the churchyard at the far end and turn left on to the road. Stay on this road, turning right along Whelp Street to return to Point **A** and rejoin the main walk at Point **5**.

Bury St Edmunds Pilgrimage

The spiritual capital of Suffolk has risen once again with a new cathedral tower.

DISTANCE 3 miles (4.8km)	**MINIMUM TIME** 1hr 30min
ASCENT/GRADIENT Negligible ▲▲▲	**LEVEL OF DIFFICULTY** +++

PATHS Town streets, gardens, meadows and riverside paths

LANDSCAPE Historic buildings of Bury St Edmunds

SUGGESTED MAP Map/town trail from tourist information centre on Angel Hill

START/FINISH Grid reference: TL 855642

DOG FRIENDLINESS Riverside path suitable for dogs

PARKING Ram Meadow pay-and-display car park

PUBLIC TOILETS At car park and Abbey Gardens

WALK 40 DIRECTIONS

Some years after King Edmund's death at Hoxne (see Walk 31), his body was moved to Beodricsworth and a shrine was built in his honour in the town which became known as Bury St Edmunds. It soon became an important place of pilgrimage and its abbey grew to be one of the most powerful in Europe. Bury, today, remains the religious capital of Suffolk, a status which has been reinforced with the building of its cathedral tower, completed in 2005. It is also a delightful town in which to stroll. On this walk you take in 1,000 years of history, from Norman flint and Elizabethan timber to Georgian brick and Victorian Bath stone, along with beautiful gardens and a short stretch along the River Lark.

Turn left out of the car park and walk past the bus garage to reach the side entrance to the Abbey Gardens. Turn right and climb to Angel Hill. This is the site of the old Bury Fair, which brought entertainers and salesmen from all over Europe until it was banned on grounds of immorality in 1871. The ivy-covered building is the Angel, mentioned by Charles Dickens in *Pickwick Papers*. Across the square are the Athenaeum Subscription Rooms, with a grand 18th-century ballroom where Dickens gave readings and where concerts still take place. On the left, the Abbey Gate is one of two surviving gateways of the old abbey, which was sacked by the townspeople in 1327 and dissolved by Henry VIII in 1539. Just inside the gateway is the world's first internet park bench, with free modem sockets for laptop computers. Beyond here are the ruins of the Norman abbey.

Turn right to walk up Abbeygate Street. When you reach the

WHAT TO LOOK OUT FOR

Don't miss the charnel house with its memorable inscriptions, including one to a nine-year-old girl struck by lightning and another to the unfortunate Sarah Lloyd, who was hanged in 1800 after being caught by 'the allurements of vice and the treacherous snares of seduction'.

building on the corner of Whiting Street, note the medieval carved beams on display in the window. Across the street, at first floor level, is a statue of St Edmund in a niche.

Turn right along Skinner Street to emerge on Cornhill opposite Moyses Hall, a Norman house from the 12th century. Turn left and left again to return to Abbeygate Street along The Traverse, passing the Nutshell, England's smallest pub, on the left. Turn right past the Corn Exchange and left along Guildhall Street, noting the 15th-century Guildhall with its flint porch. Turn left along College Lane opposite the Black Boy pub and continue on this passage past a half-timbered cottage with overhanging jetties and carved angel window frames. Keep straight ahead to cross two roads before swinging right and left on Church Walks. Turn right along Bridewell Lane and left at the end of the street to reach the Greene King brewery and a splendid Georgian playhouse, the Theatre Royal (1819), now in the hands of the National Trust, but still in use as a theatre.

WHILE YOU'RE THERE

Moyses Hall has been a private house, an inn, a prison, a police station and a parcels office but it is now a museum with displays on Bury and its past. Among the exhibits here is a gallery on crime and punishment, with gruesome mementoes of the Red Barn murder (see Walk 27) including a book bound with William Corder's skin.

Turn left opposite the theatre to arrive at St Mary's Church, where Mary Tudor, younger sister of Henry VIII, is buried. Beyond the church is the Norman Tower, part of the original abbey and now the bell tower for St Edmundsbury Cathedral. This unusual cathedral began life as a parish church and was upgraded in 1914 when the diocese of St Edmundsbury and Ipswich was created. The building of the Millennium Tower will finally make the cathedral worthy of the name and give the skyline more interest than the sugar factory.

WHERE TO EAT AND DRINK

It always feels crowded in the Nutshell, with just a couple of wooden benches and drinkers spilling out into the street. No food is served here. Greene King beers are available at the Dog and Partridge, close to Westgate Brewery, and other pubs around the town. The tea rooms in the Abbey Gardens are open in summer.

Turn right between the cathedral and the Norman Tower and cross the Great Churchyard to your right to arrive on Honey Hill opposite the Manor House Museum. Turn left here and keep to the left of the Old Shire Hall on a footpath signposted 'Moreton Hall Estate'. Cross the car park and turn right through a wooden gate into the No Man's Meadows nature reserve, passing an information board and walking through The Crankles, an area of medieval fishponds now planted with cricket bat willows. Stay on this path through water-meadows then turn right to cross a footbridge and climb some steps. Turn left to walk past the rugby ground. Turn left at the road, cross a bridge and turn left on to a bridleway that runs beside the River Lark. Keep straight ahead at a crossing on the tarmac path to return to the Abbey Gardens via a bridge.

Rowley, Poley, Hartest and Boxted

Discover a link with a well-known nursery rhyme on the rooftop of Suffolk.

DISTANCE *5 miles (8km)* MINIMUM TIME *2hrs*

ASCENT/GRADIENT *394ft (120m)* ▲▲▲ LEVEL OF DIFFICULTY ✦✦✦

PATHS *Quiet country roads, footpaths and bridleways*

LANDSCAPE *Views over Suffolk from high farmland*

SUGGESTED MAP *OS Explorer 211 Bury St Edmunds & Stowmarket*

START/FINISH *Grid reference: TL 833525*

DOG FRIENDLINESS *Keep dogs on lead*

PARKING *Hartest village hall*

PUBLIC TOILETS *None en route*

In the Poley chapel at Holy Trinity Church, Boxted, stands a life-size alabaster sculpture of Sir John Poley (1558–1638), wearing a golden frog in his ear. Historians have puzzled over the meaning of this frog, but the answer almost certainly lies in a nursery rhyme. You probably remember the rhyme from your childhood:

> *'A frog he would a-wooing go,*
> *Heigh-ho, says Rowley,*
> *A frog he would a-wooing go,*
> *Whether his mother would let him or no,*
> *With a Rowley, Poley, Gammon and Spinach,*
> *Heigh-ho says Anthony Rowley'*

Sing-song Names

The Rowleys and the Poleys were old East Anglian families whose sing-song names were too good to resist. Gammon and Spinach evolved out of the names of two other families, Bacon and Green. And the frog? This just could be a reference to Sir John Poley, who was killed in battle while fighting in France. According to legend, his horse swam back across the English Channel and made its way to Boxted Hall.

The Poleys and Weller-Poleys have lived in Boxted for more than 600 years. Many of them are buried in the family chapel, where their names are recorded on a marble scroll. The chancel of the church contains a pair of oak effigies of William Poley (died 1587), dressed in armour, his head resting on a helmet, and his wife Alice in prayer. Near by, above the altar, a stained-glass window commemorates Hugh Weller-Poley, a more recent member of the family, who was killed in action at the age of 20 in 1942.

Holy Trinity is set high among the trees overlooking the moated, half-timbered Boxted Hall. This must be one of the most delightful small churches in Suffolk. The chancel has a rare 17th-century hammerbeam roof, while the north aisle is divided into separate pews, one for the Poley family, one for their servants (the latter now houses the organ). When the church

HARTEST

was threatened with closure in the 1990s, the villagers got together to restore it. Although fewer than 100 people live in the parish, they managed to raise more than £20,000.

Glacial Erratic

Hartest, where the walk begins, has shared a priest with Boxted since 1224. This is a picture-book village set around a triangular green with thatched cottages and a fine avenue of chestnut trees. The most unusual sight is the Hartest Stone, a large glacial stone found in the neighbouring village of Somerton and dragged here on a sledge drawn by 45 horses to celebrate the Treaty of Utrecht, which awarded Gibraltar and Menorca to Britain in 1713. The nearby village sign, erected in 1990 to mark Hartest's millennium, features the stone and also a stag or hart, the original name for the village being 'hart's wood'.

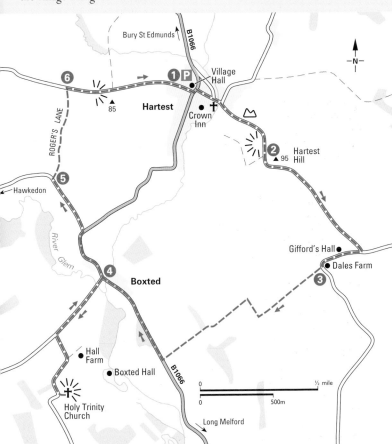

WALK 41 DIRECTIONS

❶ Turn left out of the village hall car park and cross the road to reach the village sign. Continue along the south side of the green, passing the Crown Inn and All Saints Church. Keep on this road as it bends to the right, leaving the village behind to climb Hartest Hill. Along the way you pass a peaceful burial ground.

WHERE TO EAT AND DRINK

The Crown Inn, set back from the village green in Hartest, has large gardens, a children's playground and a wide-ranging menu including fresh cod, plaice and haddock from Lowestoft. The traditional Suffolk pink coloured building was formerly the 16th-century Hartest Hall, owned by the Bishop of Ely. Refreshments are also available at Kentwell Hall in summer (see While You're There).

❷ When you reach a public footpath leading off to the right, pause at the summit of Hartest Hill to admire the extensive views over High Suffolk and Hartest nestling in its own little valley. Stay on this road for a further 0.75 mile (1.2km). Turn right when you get to the junction to reach Gifford's Hall and continue ahead until you reach the next bend in the road.

❸ When the road swings left at Dales Farm, keep straight ahead on a bridleway, which clings to hedges and field-edges as it descends towards Boxted. When you reach a road, turn right to walk into the village itself.

❹ Turn left when you see a sign to Boxted church. Cross the bridge over the River Glem and

WHAT TO LOOK OUT FOR

On an outside wall of Holy Trinity Church, to the right of the timber porch, look for the scratch dial, a simple form of sundial that would have been used to indicate the times of church services. Inside the church, look out for the plaque to Philip and Martha Hamond, erected in 1679 by Edmund Plume, 'whose wife was sister and whose sister was wife to the above Philip Hamond'.

stay on this road as it climbs out of the village. About 0.5 mile (800m) after leaving Boxted, you reach the church, hidden among the trees, with views over Boxted Hall from the churchyard. Retrace your steps into Boxted (for a short cut, you could leave this section out, but you would be missing one of the high points of the walk). Returning to the start of Point ❹, turn left, pass the electricity sub station and keep left towards Hawkedon when the road divides.

WHILE YOU'RE THERE

Kentwell Hall, just 3 miles (4.8km) away, is regarded by many as the very epitome of an Elizabethan mansion, with its mellow red-brick walls, moat and surrounding parkland. But what makes it most fascinating is that it is no stately home preserved as a museum, but a lived-in family home with ongoing restoration taking place. At certain times throughout the year, up to 250 people take part in authentic recreations of everyday Tudor life, which includes dressing and speaking as they would have 500 years ago.

❺ Approaching the first house on the left, look for a public footpath, half-hidden between tall hedges to your right. This path is known as Roger's Lane. At times it can become very muddy and overgrown, in which case a simpler alternative is to go back to the junction and return to Hartest by road. Otherwise, keep on this path as it ascends the hill.

❻ When you get to the top of Roger's Lane, turn right along the road to descend into Hartest village, with more wonderful views. The road ends at the village hall, which was erected by Thomas Weller-Poley in 1888.

The Saxons of West Stow

*Walk in the footsteps of the Anglo-Saxons
on this forest and riverside stroll.*

DISTANCE *4.25 miles (6.8km)* MINIMUM TIME *1hr 45min*

ASCENT/GRADIENT *Negligible* ▲▲▲ LEVEL OF DIFFICULTY ✦✦✦

PATHS *Country park, riverside and forest paths*

LANDSCAPE *Heathland, woodland, forest, river, lake*

SUGGESTED MAP *OS Explorer 229 Thetford Forest in the Brecks, and map of country park available from visitor centre*

START/FINISH *Grid reference: TL 800714*

DOG FRIENDLINESS *On lead in West Stow Country Park and on Forestry Commission land*

PARKING *West Stow Country Park car park*

PUBLIC TOILETS *At car park*

The reputation of the early English as crude, marauding barbarians has had to be revised following discoveries at Sutton Hoo and West Stow. It was around AD 420 that Saxon settlers from Germany sailed up the River Lark and established a village at Stowa ('special place'). The settlement, which probably consisted of about 60 people made up of two or three families and their slaves, lasted for some 200 years and its excavation has thrown new light on the Anglo-Saxon people and their way of life, forcing us to re-examine our view of the Dark Ages.

Living History

Among the finds on display in the Anglo-Saxon Centre at West Stow are bronze brooches, bone combs, amber and glass beads, silver jewellery, swords and shields, which reveal both a degree of technical sophistication and a level of contact with other cultures far greater than previously thought. What makes West Stow really interesting to visit, however, is the way the village has been reconstructed, not as an Anglo-Saxon theme park but using serious archaeological techniques in an attempt to recreate early English life as authentically as possible. Clues such as post holes in the ground and the remains of burnt-out timber buildings have allowed us to build up a vivid picture of the village, with a large communal hall surrounded by smaller houses, barns and workshops with raised floors, timber walls and thatched roofs.

Anglo-Saxons

If you can, visit West Stow over a bank holiday weekend or during the school holidays, when costumed 'Anglo-Saxons' from living history groups move into the village. (Telephone the visitor centre to check dates in advance.) Children in particular will have great fun meeting these villagers and watching them at work building fires and giving demonstrations of everything from weaving, dyeing, pottery and woodwork to jewellery-making, leatherwork and blacksmithing in the old forge.

WEST STOW COUNTRY PARK

The Anglo-Saxon village is situated inside West Stow Country Park, which means you can combine a visit with a walk for an interesting day out. The 125-acre (51ha) park was opened in 1979 on the site of a former sewage farm between the River Lark and the King's Forest. This is on the southern edge of the Brecks, a large area of dry, sandy heathland and pine forest straddling Norfolk and Suffolk. There are several short trails within the country park, but for a longer walk try this easy circuit which takes in a variety of wildlife habitats.

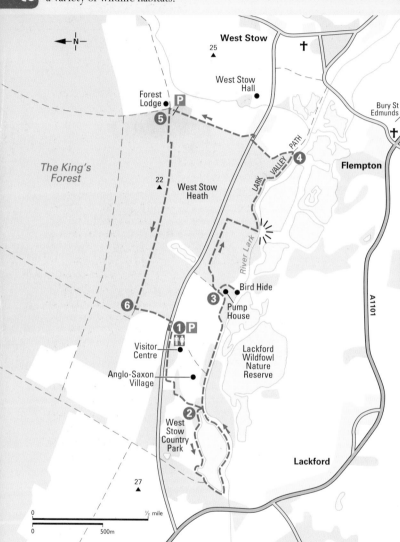

WALK 42 DIRECTIONS

❶ From the car park, follow the well-signposted nature trail that starts between the toilets and the visitor centre. The path is waymarked with red arrows and there are occasional interpretation boards describing the flora and fauna to be seen along the way.

WEST STOW COUNTRY PARK

After walking through a woody glade, you reach the open space of West Stow Heath. Pass through two gates and continue walking down to the river.

2 Turn right at a junction of paths to walk around the lake, a flooded former gravel pit used in the construction of Lakenheath airfield during World War Two. You should see ducks and Canada geese here, and great crested grebes nest on the islands in spring. Returning to the start of Point **2**, keep right along the river bank, where if you are lucky you might spot herons and kingfishers. When the nature trail turns left, keep straight ahead on a grassy riverside path, following yellow arrows. Stay on this path as it swings to the left, then climb an embankment and turn right towards an old pump house. A short diversion to the right leads to a bird hide overlooking the Lackford Wildfowl Nature Reserve.

3 Turn right at the pump house and follow the Lark Valley Path, winding through pine woods and turning sharp right to return to the river with views over a lake. Turn left here and stay close to the river as you pass behind a sewage works.

4 When you see a small weir ahead, turn left on a wide Forestry Commission track leading into West Stow village. The track briefly doubles back on itself, then swings right to run alongside the pine woods, past a barrier and behind a

group of houses to the road. Turn right, passing a 30mph sign, then go left along a tarmac lane marked by a red Forestry Commission sign (No. 205). Walk along this lane to Forest Lodge.

5 Turn left across the car park and take the path behind the notice board to enter the forest. Follow this path round to the left, then turn right where it joins a wide track. Stay on this track with yellow-topped posts as it crosses a clearing and continues through the forest. Between March and July every year, herons breed in these woodlands and it is essential to stick to the path to avoid disturbing nesting birds.

6 When you see a derelict barn at the corner of a field (just before the red Forestry Commission sign No. 209), turn left along a narrow footpath on the edge of the woods to return to the road directly opposite the car park.

Chocolate-box Cavendish

Fine views and the story of a great humanitarian in the Stour Valley.

DISTANCE *7 miles (11.3km)* MINIMUM TIME *2hrs 30min*

ASCENT/GRADIENT *311ft (95m)* ▲▲▲ LEVEL OF DIFFICULTY +++

PATHS *Field paths, bridleways, short stretches of road, 3 stiles*

LANDSCAPE *Rolling farmland of Stour Valley*

SUGGESTED MAP *OS Explorers 196 Sudbury, Hadleigh & Dedham Vale; 210 Newmarket & Haverhil*

START/FINISH *Grid reference: TL 805512 (on Explorer 196)*

DOG FRIENDLINESS *Farmland – dogs on lead*

PARKING *Cavendish High Street, near The George*

PUBLIC TOILETS *At Clare Castle Country Park*

The village green at Cavendish, with its pink thatched cottages in the shadow of a medieval church, is one of those scenes that sum up the appeal of this corner of West Suffolk. Just around the corner, in a 16th-century rectory by the duck pond, is the former home of a remarkable 20th-century figure. Sue Ryder, Baroness Ryder of Warsaw (1923–2000) was born into a large landowning family from Yorkshire and spent much of her childhood in Suffolk at their summer estate at Great Thurlow Hall. Her mother Mabel was a tireless campaigner for the rights of the poor and used to take young Sue around the slums of Leeds to teach her about poverty.

Sue Ryder Foundation

As a young woman, Sue Ryder joined the First Aid Nursing Yeomanry and later served in Poland during World War II with the top-secret Special Operations Executive, set up by Winston Churchill to organise resistance behind enemy lines. Her experience profoundly affected her and after the war she began visiting Polish prisoners and survivors of the Nazi concentration camps. In 1952 she established the Sue Ryder Foundation. A year later, using £1,000 of her own savings, she opened the first Sue Ryder home for victims of war in her mother's former house in Cavendish.

In 1959 she married Group Captain Leonard Cheshire, VC, a World War Two pilot whose experience of the devastation caused by the atomic bomb at Nagasaki led him to establish his own group of homes for disabled ex-servicemen. They lived together in two simple rooms above the Cavendish home. Sue Ryder was famous for her frugal lifestyle – she never drew a salary and dressed in clothes acquired from her own charity shops. By the time she died in October 2000, the Sue Ryder Foundation had a worldwide network of more than 60 homes for severely ill and disabled people.

This walk follows the Stour Valley Path from Cavendish to Clare, briefly entering Clare Castle Country Park and returning through Essex along the south bank of the river. For a complete look at Clare and its country park, take the longer Walk 44.

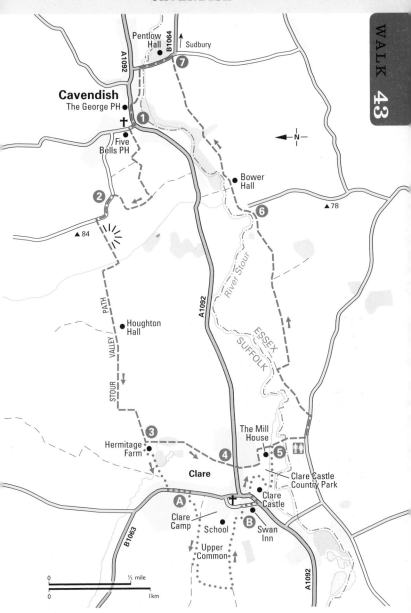

WALK 43 DIRECTIONS

1 Start at Cavendish village green. Take the path on the far side of the green past the Five Bells pub and the school, then cross the stile by the cemetery to join the Stour Valley Path. Follow this across a meadow and through a hedge, then turn left along a field-edge path that crosses a plank bridge and swings round to the right between fields and hedgerows to meet a road.

2 Turn left on to the road and walk uphill for about 0.25 mile (400m). After passing a

Overleaf: Church and pink thatched cottages in Cavendish (Walk 43)

123

solitary house, turn left on to a path along the edge of a field path with sweeping views. The path descends, then bends right and crosses a wooden bridge to emerge by a huge field. Turn right beside a hedge, then left between fields, following the Stour Valley Path waymarks to Houghton Hall (the café at the hall's health spa is signposted left). Keep straight ahead and stay on this path as it turns left and then right to drop to Hermitage Farm.

❸ Keep to the Stour Valley Path as it bends left, entering a belt of trees before reaching a lane and passing a playing field on its way to the Clare to Cavendish road.

❹ Cross the road carefully, walk across the bridge and turn left on a narrow path beside a small graveyard, signposted 'Clare Castle Country Park'. Enter the park and keep left, walking beside a stream to reach an old railway bridge. Cross the bridge and immediately take a climbing path to your left to reach a housing estate. Turn right and cross the old bridge over the railway to The Mill House and a footbridge by the old mill.

❺ Cross the bridge and walk diagonally left across a field, taking another footbridge over the River Stour to enter the county of Essex. Keep straight ahead across the field. Reaching a road, go left for 200yds (183m) before turning left on a wide bridleway leading back

down to the river. At a junction of paths by the river, turn right across the field. The track swings left behind a hedge, eventually passing a poplar grove before entering a muddy section of woodland as it meets the river once again.

❻ When you reach a lane, turn left walking past the half-timbered Bower Hall. Keep on the public bridleway for about 1 mile (1.6km) as it crosses farmland towards Pentlow Hall.

❼ Turn left on to a road and cross the bridge to return to Suffolk. On the far side of the bridge, cross a stile on the left-hand side to walk beside the river. Climb the bank on the right, cross another stile and walk through the gardens to reach the main road in Cavendish.

Clare and its Castle

A longer walk to a wool town
and a railway station inside an old castle.
See map and information panel for Walk 43

DISTANCE *8.5 miles (13.7km)* **MINIMUM TIME** *4hrs*

ASCENT/GRADIENT *394ft (120m)* ▲▲▲ **LEVEL OF DIFFICULTY** +++

PATHS *3 stiles*

WALK 44 DIRECTIONS
(Walk 43 option)

At Point ❸ on Walk 43, look for a gap in the hedge to your right, signposted 'Circular Walk'. Pass to the right of a barn then follow the farm drive and walk through Hermitage Meadow to Bridewell Street. Go left along this road for about 200yds (183m) then turn right along a wide track, Point ❹.

Cross a stile on your left into Clare Camp, the former Anglo-Saxon settlement of Erbury ('earthen fort'), now part of Lower Common. Bear right around the common towards an interpretation board, then turn right and cross another stile to return to the wide track (if you don't want to climb the stiles, just stay on the track instead).

Keep to the left of the hedge here and take a path around the fields and allotments of Upper Common. The path climbs to a summit, turns left behind a hedgerow, then left again at a junction of paths to return to Clare. Keep the church ahead of you, with glimpses of the ruined castle through the trees on the right. Pass a school playground, turn right at a farm gate and when you reach the cemetery, Point ❸, turn left to the Church of St Peter and St Paul.

Turn right along High Street. In a corner of the churchyard, notice Ancient House, built in 1473, with its carved door and window frames and elaborate pargeting. It is now a museum, open Thursday to Sunday in summer. Further along High Street, look out for the Swan Inn, which boasts perhaps the oldest pub sign in England, carved from a single piece of oak and displaying the royal coats of arms of England and France.

Turn left into Market Hill. Cross the road and enter Clare Castle Country Park along Station Road. There is plenty to do here, including nature trails, riverside walks, a playground and a small museum inside an old goods shed. Children can climb the path to the top of the castle mound for great views. Follow the path round to the right to reach the old railway station, then turn right across the Inner Bailey picnic area, passing the park centre. Walk through the car park and cross the old railway bridge, then turn left along the far bank of the New Cut to reach the old mill, Point ❺ on Walk 43.

Brandon and Thetford Forest

A pleasant riverside and forest walk on the borders of Norfolk and Suffolk.

DISTANCE 5.5 miles (8.8km)   MINIMUM TIME 2hrs

ASCENT/GRADIENT Negligible ▲▲▲   LEVEL OF DIFFICULTY ✦✦✦

PATHS Riverside and forest paths, some roads

LANDSCAPE Brandon, Thetford Forest and Little Ouse River

SUGGESTED MAP OS Explorer 229 Thetford Forest in the Brecks

START/FINISH Grid reference: TL 784864

DOG FRIENDLINESS Dogs should be kept under control in Thetford Forest Park

PARKING Market Hill car park (free), Brandon

PUBLIC TOILETS At car park and Thetford Forest Park centre

WALK 45 DIRECTIONS

Brandon lies at the heart of the Brecks, a large area of heathland and pine forest straddling north Suffolk and south Norfolk. Beneath the sandy soil lie vast amounts of flint, a fact that has played a major role in the history of the town. Flint was mined near Brandon in neolithic times, and in the 19th century more than 200 knappers were employed locally to produce gun flints for the Napoleonic Wars. Even today, many buildings in Brandon are built of flint and brick.

Prehistoric farmers used flint axes to create the large open heathland, which was kept clear for centuries by grazing rabbits and sheep. The nature of the Brecks changed for ever with the planting of Thetford Forest, Britain's largest lowland pine forest, in the 1920s. This easy-to-follow walk takes you along the Little Ouse River from Brandon to Santon Downham, returning on a forest path. Although the walk begins and ends in Suffolk, much of it is actually in Norfolk, on the north bank of the river.

From the car park, follow the signs to the town centre, emerging on Market Hill, a large square where a market is held twice a week. Cross the road here and continue along the High Street until you come to a bridge over the Little Ouse. Cross the bridge and take the first turning right along Riverside Way, then leave the road by turning right along a narrow path that runs down towards the river.

This is the start of the Little Ouse Path, a riverside footpath connecting Brandon to Thetford. Turn left along the river bank to cross a footbridge and pass a landing stage that marks the limit

---

WHERE TO EAT AND DRINK

Lunchtime options in Brandon include Collins Fish Restaurant on the High Street and the Five Bells pub on Market Hill, close to the start of the walk. Another good choice is the Ram Inn, beside the bridge over the Little Ouse. There is nowhere to eat at Santon Downham, but the village shop sells drinks and ice creams.

of navigation on the river. Stay on this path for about 2.5 miles (4km) as it follows the twists and turns of the river, with views of marshes, pine forest and meadows on the far bank. This is a very peaceful stretch of the walk and the silence is only disturbed by the splashing of ducks or the occasional sound of a train on the railway line that runs parallel to the river.

WHAT TO LOOK OUT FOR

Approaching Santon Downham from the river, you pass an attractive terrace of flint-faced bungalows on your right. These old cottages are typical of the building style of the Brecks, using the flint stones found in the chalk below the soil.

Eventually the river straightens out before sweeping round to the right in a wide arc. When you reach a bridge, climb the steps and turn right over the bridge into the village of Santon Downham. This lovely village, deep in the forest, is the headquarters of Thetford Forest Park. In 1668, the entire village was engulfed by a sand storm, once a common occurrence in these parts.

Pass the forest centre and the village shop, and continue up the hill to St Mary's Church, otherwise known as the Church in the Forest. Turn right opposite the church to walk briefly alongside the road

to Brandon, facing the village green. When the road bends left, keep straight ahead on a surfaced track leading to a telephone box and the village hall. When the track ends, continue straight ahead on a footpath into the forest.

Stay on this path as it bends to the right and crosses a wide sandy track. Shortly afterwards, you pass a metal barrier and follow the path round to the left. The path winds gently through the forest, passing a campsite and another metal barrier before reaching the stables and paddocks of a riding school. Follow the track past the school, but when the track bends left, turn right along a narrow path between the paddocks and the woods.

The route from here back to Brandon is straightforward. Stay on this path as it gradually widens to become a track with a flint-faced wall on the left. The track, known as Gashouse Drove, continues all the way to the High Street, passing a housing estate and then a group of large modern houses on the left. Turn left at the High Street to return to the car park at the start of the walk.

WHILE YOU'RE THERE

Grimes Graves, 2 miles (3.2km) north of Santon Downham, has been described as the oldest industrial site in Europe. Visitors can go deep down into the shafts of a prehistoric mine to see where flint was gathered more than 4,000 years ago. To learn more about the area's history of flint mining and forestry, visit the Brandon Heritage Centre on George Street, open on summer weekends. Children will enjoy Brandon Country Park, with its tree trail, forest walks, walled garden, parkland and lake, and the High Lodge Forest Centre in Thetford Forest Park, which makes a great family day out with its adventure course, maze, bike hire, cycle trails, waymarked walks and hands-on nature activities for kids.

The Skies Above Mildenhall

*Giant American aircraft can be seen overhead
on this peaceful walk in the Lark Valley.*

DISTANCE *5.5 miles (8.8km)*   MINIMUM TIME *2hrs*

ASCENT/GRADIENT *Negligible* ▲▲▲   LEVEL OF DIFFICULTY +++

PATHS *Bridleway and riverside footpath, town streets, 2 stiles*

LANDSCAPE *Mildenhall town and valley of River Lark*

SUGGESTED MAP *OS Explorer 226 Ely & Newmarket*

START/FINISH *Grid reference: TL 713745*

DOG FRIENDLINESS *Dogs should be kept under control*

PARKING *Jubilee car park, Mildenhall*

PUBLIC TOILETS *At car park*

The sight and sound of aircraft taking off and landing will be a constant backdrop to this walk in the shadow of Mildenhall airfield, the headquarters of the 3rd United States Air Force in Europe.

RAF Mildenhall opened as a British bomber base in October 1934. Just four days after its opening, it was the scene of one of the most dramatic events in its history as King George V and Queen Mary attended the start of the England to Australia air race, held as part of the city of Melbourne's centenary celebrations. The early leader was Amy Johnson in a De Havilland DH88 Comet, but the race was won in another DH88 by Charles Scott and Tom Campbell Black, who covered the 11,300 miles (18,180km) in a time of 70 hours, 54 minutes and 18 seconds. Rather less impressive was a Fairey Fox biplane, which reached Melbourne 116 days after the race began.

During World War II, Mildenhall was one of a number of Suffolk airfields used by Allied forces – there were others at Lakenheath, Lavenham, Flixton, Eye, Mendlesham, Metfield and Parham. Wellington bombers from Mildenhall engaged the German Navy within a day of war being declared, and throughout the war they continued to attack German targets as well as providing cover for Allied troops during the D-Day landings in Normandy and the evacuation of Dunkirk. In all, some 200 aircraft from Mildenhall were lost and 1,900 men killed in action during the course of the war.

The American presence at Mildenhall began in 1950 and it is now the gateway to Britain for more than 100,000 military personnel each year.

Mildenhall Treasure

Mildenhall's other claim to fame is the Mildenhall Treasure, the most significant hoard of Roman silverware ever discovered in Britain. The story of its discovery is almost as remarkable as the treasure itself. In January 1943, Gordon Butcher was ploughing at West Row when he found a metal bowl buried in the ground. He showed it to his boss, Sydney Ford, who happened to collect antiques. Between them they dug up 34 pieces of blackened silverware, including plates, spoons, goblets and bowls, and a great dish almost 2ft (60cm) in diameter, richly decorated with scenes from Roman mythology. Ford took the objects home, cleaned them up and kept them on his mantelpiece for three years until eventually someone persuaded him to take them to the police. In 1946 the hoard was declared treasure trove and given to the British Museum. Ford and Butcher received a reward of £1,000 each.

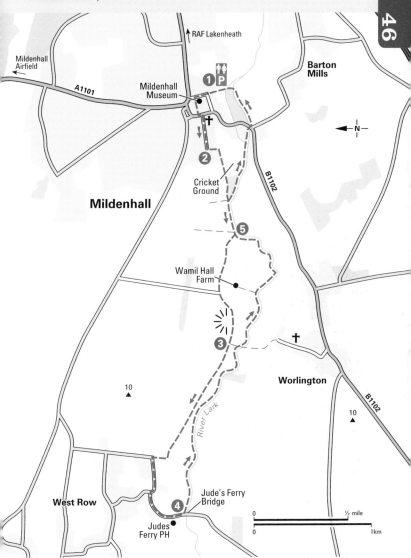

WALK 46 DIRECTIONS

❶ From the Jubilee car park, walk up King Street as far as the Mildenhall Museum, in an old flint-faced building on the left. Turn left along Market Street to enter Market Place, with its parish pump and 16th-century Market Cross. Cross High Street, turn left and immediately right along Church Walk to walk through the churchyard and continue along a narrow road.

2 At the end of the road, turn left and follow the bridleway signs around to the right past the cricket ground. The path is shady and tree-lined at first, then it passes behind a cottage and continues across the fields on a track leading to Wamil Hall Farm. After passing the farm buildings, keep straight ahead on a concrete lane that bends left and right towards a large house enclosed by a brick wall. There are views across the river to Worlington church and of Mildenhall airfield to your right.

WHERE TO EAT AND DRINK

Judes Ferry pub, at the half-way point of the walk, has real ales and home-cooked food in a delightful setting, with riverside gardens, mooring for boats, and an adventure playground for kids. Alternatively, you can pick up picnic provisions or filled rolls from Barleycorn or A Taste of the Best, both on the Market Place at Mildenhall.

3 Keep straight ahead on a grassy field-edge path and continue for 0.75 mile (1.2km) until the path turns sharply right to meet a road at West Row. Turn left here, passing a group of bungalows. When the road bends right, take the second left into Ferry Lane which leads down to the River Lark at Jude's Ferry.

4 Walk past the pub and take the steps down to the river to turn left on to the riverside path beneath the bridge. This path will take you all the way back to Mildenhall. The walk back is completely different in character even though you are rarely more than 0.25 mile (400m) from your outward route. Previously it was all wide open spaces and skies, now it is the river that dominates and you are more likely to see

WHILE YOU'RE THERE

The Mildenhall Museum contains a complete replica of the Mildenhall Treasure, the originals of which are in the British Museum in London. There are also galleries devoted to local history, ecology and RAF Mildenhall.

herons than military planes. Keep to the river bank, passing through kissing gates either side of a garden and climbing to a bridge behind Wamil Hall Farm. Eventually the path turns away from the river to briefly rejoin the outward route.

5 Turn right at the cottage and when the path divides after 300yds (274m), keep right beside the river, passing behind the cricket ground. When the river divides, cross a bridge to reach an island by a small lock. Climb to the road bridge and cross to the south bank, then turn left along a gravel drive that soon becomes a riverside path. Cross the river over a pair of arched bridges and bear left at the playing fields to return to the start of the walk.

WHAT TO LOOK OUT FOR

Aircraft enthusiasts can try to identify American warplanes in the skies above Mildenhall. The base itself is understandably off limits, but for a close-up look at F15 fighter/bombers and other military planes, you can visit the observation area at nearby RAF Lakenheath, signposted off the A1065 from Mildenhall to Brandon.

The Estate Villages of Thurlow

An easy walk across high farmland belonging to one of Suffolk's largest agricultural estates.

DISTANCE 3.5 miles (5.7km) MINIMUM TIME 1hr 30min

ASCENT/GRADIENT 164ft (50m) ▲▲▲ LEVEL OF DIFFICULTY ✦✦✦

PATHS Country roads, meadows and field-edge paths, 6 stiles

LANDSCAPE Gently rolling farmland

SUGGESTED MAP OS Explorer 210 Newmarket & Haverhill

START/FINISH Grid reference: TL 678502

DOG FRIENDLINESS Mostly on lead on farmland

PARKING Great Thurlow Reading Room or village hall

PUBLIC TOILETS None en route

Haverhill, in the south-west corner of Suffolk, gets rather a bad press. It has none of the immediate appeal of the nearby wool towns and its relentless expansion during the last 50 years has diluted any sense of history it may have had and led to endless jibes about 'London overspill'. Yet as those of us who live near Haverhill know, this is not entirely fair. The town is still surrounded by lovely countryside and by villages that have hardly changed for hundreds of years.

The Vestey Family

This walk is centred on the twin villages of Great and Little Thurlow, which have been called the last feudal villages in Suffolk. Most of the land belongs to the Thurlow Estate, which owns 17,000 acres (6,880ha) of prime arable farmland in Suffolk, Essex and Cambridgeshire, as well as a herd of dairy cattle. Much of this is in the hands of Edmund Vestey of Little Thurlow Hall, whose grandfather made his fortune in the late 19th century when he established Union Cold Storage in Liverpool to import cheap meat from Australia and became known as 'Mr Spam'. The Vestey family is now one of the richest in Britain, with assets of over £700 million and valued at No. 101 on the Sunday Times Rich List in 2008.

According to his biography in *Who's Who*, Edmund Vestey was educated at Eton, owns two estates in Scotland, is a member of the Cavalry and Guards Club and joint master of the Thurlow Hunt, one of the oldest hunts in the country. His son George lives in Great Thurlow Hall. The Vestey family play a key role in local affairs and have provided the villages with facilities including a recreation ground, but there are those who feel it is inappropriate that so many people should be dependent on the estate both for housing and for work.

Newspaper Business

The Vesteys were not the first great landowning family in Thurlow. Sir Stephen Soame (1544–1619), who built the first Little Thurlow Hall, was Lord Mayor of London. It was he who erected the almshouses for 'eight

133

single persons of honest life and conversation', and the old schoolhouse for the teaching of Latin to boys, both of which are now private homes. A more recent lord of the manor was W H Smith (1825–91) of Great Thurlow Hall, who took over his father's newspaper business and turned it into a household name by securing the rights to sell newspapers and books at railway stations. He later became First Lord of the Treasury and Leader of the House of Commons and is remembered in Thurlow, appropriately enough, by the reading room that he gave to the village.

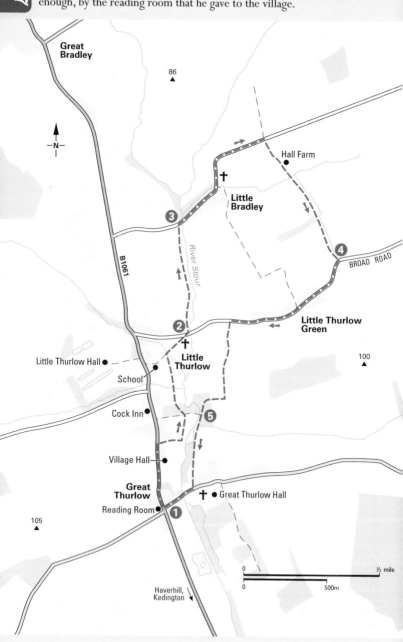

WALK 47 DIRECTIONS

1 Walk north from the Reading Room along the main street, passing the post office and the village hall, then turn right on a narrow path between the houses. Cross a stile and bear left across a meadow to reach another stile. At a junction of paths, go straight ahead across a wide track and keep left to cross two more meadows, each with stiles. Walk behind the school and bear right to pass through a gate. Cross a concrete footbridge and stay on the fenced-off path to reach St Peter's Church, Little Thurlow.

2 Walk through the churchyard and turn left to cross the road and continue on a narrow footpath beside the River Stour. The path is lined with hedges at first but you soon reach open fields. Keep to the right to walk beside the river. Although it rises only a short distance away, the Stour has already gathered pace though it is nothing like the river you will see downstream at Sudbury, Flatford or Shotley Gate.

3 When you come to a weir, turn right along the road into Little Bradley and follow it round to the left to All Saints Church, whose round tower dates to the early 11th century. The road now bends right and climbs gently between farmland to the left and meadows to the right. Turn right at a footpath sign along a farm drive. Walk past the stables and barns of Hall Farm, then go through

WHAT TO LOOK OUT FOR

In spring and summer you may see pheasant coops at some of the farms. The Thurlow Estate has its own pheasant shoot and gamekeepers are employed to rear pheasants and partridges and to manage the land for their conservation.

a gate to cross a meadow. Leaving the meadow through another gate, keep straight ahead alongside a hedge to reach a road.

4 Turn right to walk along Broad Road into the hamlet of Little Thurlow Green. After passing the green, walk downhill past modern houses and the thatched Old Inn. Before you reach the thatched pink cottage, turn left on to a concrete farm track with a hedge to your right. The path passes a sewage works then turns right and left around a field to enter a belt of woodland beside the River Stour.

5 Keep straight ahead when you see an arched footbridge across the river to your right. Cross a stile and bear right around a meadow, then pass through a gate to enter a small graveyard opposite Great Thurlow church. Turn right at the road, alongside the high brick wall of Great Thurlow Hall, and cross the river to the start of the walk.

WHILE YOU'RE THERE

The nearby village of Kedington is worth a visit to see the Church of St Peter and St Paul, situated on a ridge overlooking the Stour Valley and sometimes described as the 'cathedral of West Suffolk'. Among the interesting features of this surprisingly large parish church are a Saxon cross in the chancel and a three-tier pulpit, complete with a 'sermon-timer' to prevent the priest from droning on for too long!

Moulton and Three Churches

An enjoyable walk in rolling downland on the Cambridgeshire / Suffolk border.

DISTANCE 6.5 miles (10.4km)   MINIMUM TIME 3hrs

ASCENT/GRADIENT 295ft (90m) ▲▲▲   LEVEL OF DIFFICULTY +++

PATHS Field-edge, cross-field and woodland paths, 9 stiles

LANDSCAPE Downland, farmland, woodland and River Kennett

SUGGESTED MAP OS Explorer 210 Newmarket & Haverhill

START/FINISH Grid reference: TL 696644

DOG FRIENDLINESS Livestock – dogs on lead

PARKING Moulton village hall

PUBLIC TOILETS None en route

The walk is known locally as the Three Churches Walk, as it takes in the three churches at Moulton, Gazeley and Dalham. Much of the walk follows the Icknield Way, an ancient trail dating back to the time of the Iceni tribe, whose warrior-queen, Boudicca, ruled East Anglia in the 1st century AD. The original trail ran from Norfolk to Wiltshire and is thought to be Britain's oldest road. The modern Icknield Way path begins at Knettishall Heath and is waymarked with the sign of an axe.

This is horse racing country, just a few short gallops from Newmarket. Look out for thoroughbred horses at the Gazeley Stud, or grazing on the village green at Moulton. Don't be surprised to hear locals discussing the latest racing gossip or tips in the village pubs.

Moulton, where the walk begins, is best known for its 15th-century packhorse bridge, on the old cart road from Cambridge to Bury St Edmunds. It's built of flint with four arches lined in brick. The parapet walls were built low to allow the horses' packs to swing clear. The River Kennett flows underneath the bridge, though it's now little more than a trickle.

Dalham is the most attractive of the three villages. Some three-quarters of the houses are thatched, more than anywhere else in Suffolk. Behind the church, Dalham Hall was built for the Bishop of Ely in 1704, with instructions that Ely Cathedral should be visible from the upper floors. Unfortunately, a fire in 1957 means that the hall has been reduced to two storeys and the view of the cathedral has been lost. One of the previous owners of Dalham Hall was Cecil Rhodes (1853–1902), the Victorian empire-builder and founder of Rhodesia (now Zimbabwe), who died before he could live in the hall. There are memorials to members of his family in a corner of St Mary's churchyard. A visit to the church gives fascinating glimpses into Dalham's aristocratic and social history. Among the squires of Dalham recalled in stone are Sir Martin Stuteville, who 'visited the American world with Francis Drake', and his ancestor Thomas Stuteville, who 'kept hospitalitye in the manor place… and had 15 children.' There are also memorials to members of the Affleck family, from whom the village pub takes its name, and to their faithful servants.

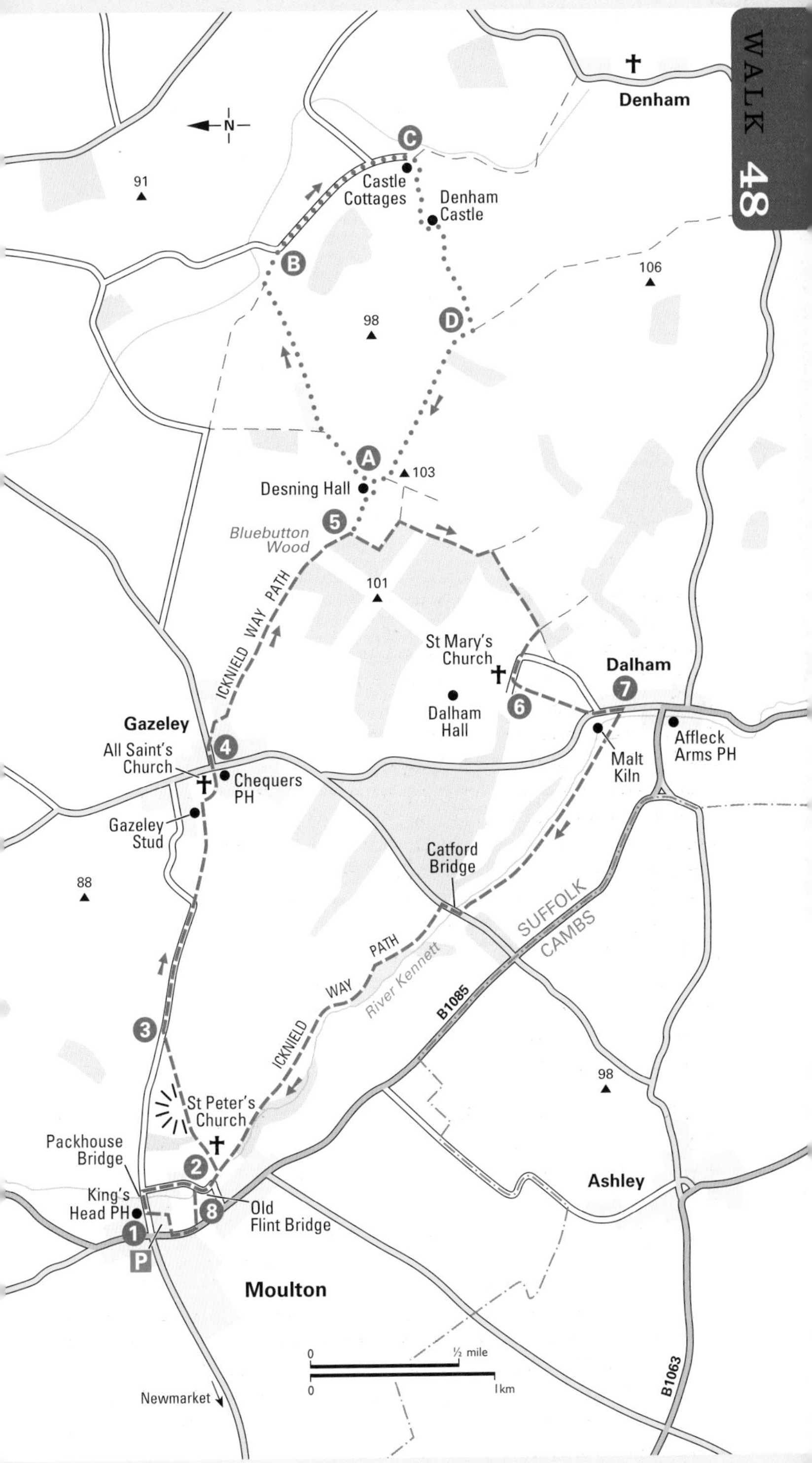

Denham ✝

← N →

91 ▲

C
Castle Cottages

Denham Castle

B

98 ▲

106 ▲

D

A

Desning Hall ▲ 103

5

Bluebutton Wood

ICKNIELD WAY PATH

101 ▲

St Mary's Church ✝

Dalham

7

Gazeley

All Saint's Church ✝

4

Chequers PH

Gazeley Stud

Dalham Hall ●

6

Malt Kiln

Affleck Arms PH

88 ▲

Catford Bridge

SUFFOLK
CAMBS

98 ▲

3

PATH

ICKNIELD WAY

River Kennett

B1085

St Peter's Church ✝

Packhouse Bridge

King's Head PH

2

8

Old Flint Bridge

Ashley

1
P

Moulton

Newmarket ←

0 .... ½ mile
0 .... 1km

B1063

WALK 48

WALK 48 DIRECTIONS

1 Turn right out of the village hall car park along Bridge Street, passing the King's Head pub on your way to the packhorse bridge. Cross the bridge and turn right along Brookside, walking beside the River Kennett. Just before the Old Flint Bridge, notice the old rectory school on your left, dating from 1849. Keep on this road until you reach the churchyard.

2 Go through the gate to enter the churchyard and pass St Peter's Church. Cross a stile behind the church and walk up through the trees to another stile at the top. Bear right across the fields. On clear days, Ely Cathedral is visible on the horizon to your left.

WHERE TO EAT AND DRINK

There are pubs in all three villages. The Affleck Arms in Dalham is an attractive thatched pub serving home-cooked food in the bar and at tables outside by the river. Alternatively, for a picnic, the post office in Moulton sells filled rolls and locally made pies.

3 Reaching a road, turn right. Keep straight ahead when the road bends, walking between the hedges of the Gazeley Stud, where mares and foals can be seen. Continue on this path to All Saints Church and walk around the rear of the church to emerge by the Gazeley village sign and the Chequers pub.

4 Walk down Higham Road, opposite the church, and bear right following the Icknield Way waymarks at Tithe Close. Walk between the houses and follow this path across the fields and into Bluebutton Wood. Where the path turns sharply right, look for a footbridge in the hedge to your left. (This is the start of Walk 49.)

5 Keep on the Icknield Way as it winds through two more woods, emerging beside a wide field. Walk along the edge of the field, up through the trees to reach a crossroads. Turn right here and climb to St Mary's Church, with Dalham Hall visible behind.

6 Pass through the metal kissing gate opposite the church and walk down through an avenue of chestnut trees to Dalham village. Go through a kissing gate and turn left, noting the large conical red-brick malt kiln standing beside the road. If you are ready for lunch, a short walk along this road leads to the Affleck Arms.

7 Cross the white footbridge to your right and follow this path beside the River Kennett. Reaching a road, turn right across Catford Bridge. Now turn left on a wide bridleway to return to Moulton at St Peter's Church.

8 Cross the Old Flint Bridge and walk across the green to reach Dalham Road. Turn right along this road. A gate opposite the post office leads to the recreation ground and back to the village hall.

WHILE YOU'RE THERE

Just north of Moulton, at a junction on the B1506, lies the grave of Joseph, an unknown gypsy boy who hanged himself after he was accused of stealing a sheep. At one time, suicides were refused burial in the churchyard and were buried at crossroads to prevent their spirits from wandering. The tombstone has become a shrine and flowers are often placed there by punters hoping for luck on their way to Newmarket races.

And On To

Denham Castle

Wide open countryside, superb views and the site of a ruined castle.
See map and information panel for Walk 48

DISTANCE 3 miles (4.8km)   MINIMUM TIME 1hr 15min
ASCENT/GRADIENT 197ft (60m) ▲▲▲   LEVEL OF DIFFICULTY ✦✦✦

WALK 49 DIRECTIONS
(Walk 48 option)

This short extension to Walk 48 takes you into some of the highest countryside in Suffolk, with sweeping views and vast, lonely skies. Although the Three Churches Walk is justifiably popular, once you have left the main walk you are unlikely to meet many other walkers here. There are no facilities on the route, so take plenty of water and a snack.

At Point ❺ on the main walk, cross the footbridge through the hedge on your left to reach a field-edge path, which can become overgrown with nettles. Turn right along this path and head for the farm buildings at Desning Hall, Point ❹. Turn right to walk through the farmyard and then go left, bearing around to the right on a concrete lane that leads to a group of flint cottages.

Fork right at the telephone box and walk past the cottages, emerging on to a bridleway where you keep straight ahead. At a junction of paths, keep to the right beside a field-edge. Reaching a gap in the hedge, Point ❸, leave the bridleway and walk through the gap on to a tarmac road. Stay on this road for 0.75 mile (1.2km). When the main road bends left, keep straight on towards Castle Farm.

Arriving at Castle Cottages, Point ❸, turn right to follow the edge of an apple orchard around the farmhouse. Keep to the yellow waymarks. At the end of the orchard, a thick clump of trees to your left hides the ruins of Denham Castle, a Norman motte-and-bailey castle built 330ft (100m) above sea level. The castle was given to William Marshall, Earl of Pembroke, by Richard I in the 12th century.

WHAT TO LOOK OUT FOR

Fallow deer were introduced to Suffolk in Norman times. The owners of Castle Farm, the Gliksten family, maintain the Denham herd of fallow deer, supplying venison to many London restaurants.

Continue on this path as it runs between fields, briefly entering a wood. Reaching a gap in the hedgerow, Point ❹, turn right on to a wide bridleway that swings left, then immediately right to return to Desning Hall. When this reaches a road, turn right. Retrace your steps through the farmyard and along the field-edge path to return to Point ❺ on Walk 48.

Newmarket's Sport of Kings

A quick canter through the world of horse racing.

DISTANCE *3 miles (4.8km)*   MINIMUM TIME *1hr 30min*

ASCENT/GRADIENT *131ft (40m)* ▲▲▲   LEVEL OF DIFFICULTY +++

PATHS *Town streets and surfaced horse ways*

LANDSCAPE *Newmarket town and heath*

SUGGESTED MAP *Map from tourist information centre, Palace House*

START/FINISH *Grid reference: TL 644633*

DOG FRIENDLINESS *Not very suitable*

PARKING *All Saints Road pay-and-display car park, near Palace House*

PUBLIC TOILETS *In cemetery and the Rookery shopping centre*

WALK 50 DIRECTIONS

Newmarket has been the capital of British horse racing ever since James I moved his summer court here in 1605 and established the town as the home of the sporting fraternity. Long before that, Queen Boudicca used to race her chariots across Newmarket Heath, but it was the royal patronage of the Stuart kings which made Newmarket the place it is today. The town is utterly devoted to racing, with farriers, saddlers and bookmakers taking the place of more conventional shops. With over 2,000 thoroughbred horses based here in training, no one could ever accuse Newmarket of being a one-horse town.

This walk takes in many of the sights associated with horse racing. Start at Palace House, where the tourist information centre is housed in a wing of Charles II's palace. It was Charles, a keen rider, who did more than anyone to put Newmarket on the map and his twice yearly visits established a pattern of spring and autumn race meetings which continues to this day. Walk up Palace Street towards a white house with shutters. This is Nell Gwynne's House, where the King installed his favourite mistress.

> ### WHERE TO EAT AND DRINK
> Coffee & Co, near the start of the walk, offers a varied menu of quiches and panini at outdoor tables in summer. There are several pubs on High Street, as well as the Bushel in the Rookery Centre. There is also a good café inside the National Horseracing Museum.

Turn right along High Street towards the clock tower. Before reaching it, turn right along Rous Road, passing some attractive gabled cottages. At the end of the road, turn right into Old Station Road and walk past the Rous Memorial Cottages, formerly almshouses for retired jockeys.

Across the street you see Warren Hill and the famous 'gallops' where the horses train each morning. The training grounds are closed to pedestrians until 1pm each day but after this time you can follow the exercise track on the left to Moulton Road. Several of the top trainers have their stables on Moulton Road, including Henry Cecil at Warren Place and Sir Mark Prescott at Heath House. Before 1pm, you will have to return along Old Station Road and take the alley between Nos. 13 and 15, emerging on Moulton Road opposite the farriers Curtis and Sons. Turn left along Moulton Road to return to the clock tower.

Cross the road and walk down the right-hand side of High Street. After 200yds (183m), turn right along an alley into the Rookery shopping centre. On your left is the Bushel pub, where Charles II is thought to have attended cock fights. Bear left at the library and right across Market Place. Cross the road just beyond a relief sculpture of a horse, and bear right along The Watercourse on a horse way behind a large white house. Behind the high wall to your left are the Hastings Centre, an equine swimming pool and therapy clinic. Turn left when at a junction and climb to the top of the street. Turn left and walk downhill as far as the Methodist chapel. Cross the road here and turn right on another horse way to St Mary's Church. Bear left through the churchyard and keep straight ahead on Fitzroy Street, passing the Memorial

WHILE YOU'RE THERE

The National Horseracing Museum has displays on the history of racing as well as a hands-on gallery where you can ride on a simulated racehorse and try on racing silks. The museum also organises equine tours of Newmarket, some of which take place on race days and include advice on betting.

Gardens, a theatre and a real tennis court. At the end of the street, turn left into Black Bear Lane past a large horse requisites shop opposite the entrance to Fitzroy Stables.

Turn right up High Street. When you reach the Cooper Memorial drinking fountain, fork right along Birdcage Walk to arrive at Newmarket Heath, with views of the Rowley Mile racecourse and Millennium Grandstand.

WHAT TO LOOK OUT FOR

A white cross in the cemetery marks the grave of Fred Archer (1857–86), perhaps the greatest jockey of all time, who was 13-times champion jockey before shooting himself at the age of 29 after his wife died in childbirth and he grew increasingly depressed at his inability to keep his weight down. The fatal revolver is on display in the museum.

Cross the main road to enter the cemetery and follow the path to the left, passing the chapel and leaving via the main gate. Cross Dullingham Road and walk down High Street to the next corner, where you will see Queensberry House, headquarters of the British Bloodstock Agency. Turn right and then left along a private road, passing Gibson Saddlers, suppliers of racing silks to the Queen.

At the foot of this road, a short detour right leads to Tattersalls, the leading equine auctioneers. Otherwise, turn left to High Street and turn right at the traffic-lights. After the post office, you come to the Jockey Club, where the rules of racing are administered, and the National Horseracing Museum. Just beyond the museum, turn right towards Moons toyshop and go left along a passage to the start.

Walking in Safety

All these walks are suitable for any reasonably fit person,
but less experienced walkers should try the easier walks first.
Route finding is usually straightforward, but you will find that
an Ordnance Survey map is a useful addition to the route maps
and descriptions.

RISKS

Although each walk here has been researched with a view to
minimising the risks to the walkers who follow its route, no walk in
the countryside can be considered to be completely free from risk.
Walking in the outdoors will always require a degree of common
sense and judgement to ensure that it is as safe as possible.

● Be particularly careful on cliff paths and in upland terrain,
  where the consequences of a slip can be very serious.

● Remember to check tidal conditions before walking on the
  seashore.

● Some sections of route are by, or cross, busy roads. Take care
  and remember traffic is a danger even on minor country lanes.

● Be careful around farmyard machinery and livestock, especially
  if you have children with you.

● Be aware of the consequences of changes in the weather and
  check the forecast before you set out. Carry spare clothing and
  a torch if you are walking in the winter months. Remember the
  weather can change very quickly at any time of the year, and
  in moorland and heathland areas, mist and fog can make route
  finding much harder. Don't set out in these conditions unless
  you are confident of your navigation skills in poor visibility. In
  summer remember to take account of the heat and sun; wear a
  hat and carry spare water.

● On walks away from centres of population you should carry a
  whistle and survival bag. If you do have an accident requiring the
  emergency services, make a note of your position as accurately
  as possible and dial 999.

COUNTRYSIDE CODE

● Be safe, plan ahead and follow any signs.

● Leave gates and property as you find them.

● Protect plants and animals and take your litter home.

● Keep dogs under close control.

● Consider other people.

For more information visit www.countrysideaccess.gov.uk/things_
to_know/countryside_code